AF382474

Akariza Laurette Annely

REBOUNCE

TRANS GENERATIONAL RESILIENCE IN RWANDA

RESILIENCE FROM ASHES

Printing and distribution on behalf of the author:

Inzozi Publisher, Pforzheimer Strasse 5, 76275 Ettlingen, Germany

Contents

Foreword

It is with great pleasure and admiration that I write this foreword for Akariza Laurette Annely's remarkable book, "Rebounce." In these pages, Akariza takes us on a poignant and inspiring journey through the concept of transgenerational resilience, drawing upon individual experiences of survivors and Rwanda's profound story of reconstruction and healing of nation after the Genocide against the Tutsi in 1994.

"Rebounce" is not just a book; it is a testament to the indomitable human spirit and the power of resilience in the face of unimaginable adversity. Through her words, Akariza invites us to delve into the depths of Rwanda's history, where the resilience of survivors has been a beacon of hope and a testament to the strength of the human soul.

As we navigate through the pages of "Rebounce," we are confronted to the harsh realities of Rwanda's past, where prejudice, discrimination, and hatred led to unspeakable atrocities. However, amidst the darkness, Akariza shines a light on the resilience of the Rwandan people, who, through their unwavering courage and determination, have emerged stronger and more united.

"Rebounce" is not only a reflection on Rwanda's past but also a beacon of hope for the future. It challenges us to reflect on our own lives and the resilience we possess within us. It reminds us that no matter how difficult the circumstances, there is always a way to rise up and overcome.The book is a great contribution serving as a good reference for different disciplines History, sociology, politics and clinical psychology as well as a contribution to transitional justice, memory and identity literature.

It serves a s a good reference for pedagogy of resilience for young people at different levels in secondary schools. Easy to read with simple definitions of concepts, defined from testimonies of "ordinary" people other than academic. This gives to the book a credibility to be a contribution to decolonial studies with local experiences, a basis for knowledge production. I am sure the shortcomings in the book will be recognized and will be an inspiration for deeper and more contribution to this important thematic area.

I commend Akariza for her courage in sharing this important story with the world. "Rebounce" is a testament to her dedication to preserving memory and ensuring that the lessons of Rwanda are never forgotten. It is a call to action for all of us to stand up against prejudice and discrimination and to embrace the power of resilience in our own lives.

I am honored to have had the opportunity to read "Rebounce," and I am confident that it will inspire and enlighten readers around the world. May it serve as a reminder that, even in our darkest moments, there is always a path to rebounce and rise up.

Dr Eric Ndushabandi *is proud Mentor and Professor of Political science to Laurette with Expertise in Post-conflict reconstruction processes* and resilience.

PROLOGUE

Before embarking on the journey that is this book, Rebounce, I want to share a piece of my story with you. A story of trials and tribulations, of failures and resilience, and above all, a story that transformed me into the person I am today.

You see, I've always been drawn to the power of words and storytelling. From a young age, I dreamt of writing books that would touch people's hearts and make a difference in their lives. But, like many dreams, it took time and numerous setbacks before I found my path.

Before Rebounce, there was "Wet under the Rainbow." It was my first published work, a collection of stories from the youth of Rwanda. These stories were a reflection of their struggles, their journey to heal, and the generational trauma they carried from the Genocide against Tutsi 1994. I penned those words when I was just 18, balancing the demands of high school with the passion to give voice to those who needed it most.

In those early days, I had no mentor, no guidebook on how to write and publish a book. I stumbled through the process, making mistakes, facing rejections, and wrestling with self-doubt. But despite the hurdles, "Wet under the Rainbow" became a reality, and it gave me a newfound purpose.

People began to reach out to me, strangers whose lives had intersected with the characters in my book. They'd say, "I don't know if you know me, but after reading your book, that David in your story is me." It was then that I realized the true power of storytelling—to connect us, to reveal our shared humanity.

Yet, as much as I wanted to shine a light on transgenerational trauma and the struggles of youth, I was unprepared for the emotional weight of their stories. I didn't anticipate the sleepless nights and tear-stained pages as I absorbed their pain. I felt the weight of their expectations, the belief that I was strong and wise. But in reality, I was just a young writer, carrying the burden of their stories alone.

It was in those moments of vulnerability that I discovered my own strength. I chose not to let the weight of the stories crush me but instead to use it as fuel for a greater purpose. In the midst of their pain, I found resilience—the indomitable spirit of youth who refused to succumb to the shadows of their past.

And so, the idea for Rebounce was born. In October 2022, I decided that it was time to share not only the stories of struggle but also the stories of triumph. To tell you, dear reader, about the incredible resilience I witnessed in the youth of Rwanda and how they bounced back from adversity.

As you embark on this journey through Rebounce, remember this: what doesn't kill you doesn't have to break you. It can make you stronger, more resilient, and more determined than ever before. There's no time to delay; you can always bounce back from whatever has laid you low. So, open your heart and mind, for within these pages, you'll discover the unbreakable spirit of those who chose to Rebounce.

CHAPTER 1: The Resilience Recipe: Ingredients of Overcoming Adversity

In this book, titled "Rebounce," we embark on a profound and deeply moving exploration of the concept of transgenerational resilience within the heart-wrenching context of the survivors of the Genocide against the Tutsi. This collection of narratives, reflections, and insights represents a powerful testament to the enduring strength, resilience, and determination that have been passed down from one generation to the next, like a torch lighting the way through the darkest of times.

The Genocide against the Tutsi, a dark chapter in human history, left an indelible mark, characterized by unimaginable atrocities and unfathomable suffering. It is a chapter that should never be forgotten, a testament to the capacity for cruelty that can be unleashed when hatred and intolerance go unchecked. However, amid the shadows of that harrowing period, there emerged a resilient spirit—a spirit that refused to be extinguished.

The survivors of the Genocide, individuals who bore witness to unspeakable horrors, have not only found ways to heal and rebuild their own lives but have also imparted invaluable lessons of resilience to their children and future generations. Through their unwavering determination to rise above the horrors they witnessed, they have sown the seeds of hope, strength, and survival in the hearts of their descendants.

"Rebounce" delves deeply into the remarkable journeys of transgenerational resilience. It casts a spotlight on the survivors' experiences and the subsequent intergenerational transmission of strength and healing. We traverse the emotional landscapes of these individuals through personal narratives that lay bare their innermost thoughts, fears, and hopes. We engage in illuminating interviews that capture the essence of their experiences, and we analyze their stories through the lens of scholarly perspectives to gain a holistic understanding of this profound phenomenon.

At its core, "Rebounce" is a heartfelt tribute to the survivors. It pays homage to their indomitable spirit and their commitment to ensuring that the atrocities they endured are never forgotten. It is a living testament to their extraordinary ability to bounce back from unimaginable trauma, to rebuild shattered lives, and to continue their journey with resilience that is nothing short of inspirational.

Within the pages of "Rebounce," we strive to shed light on the multifaceted dimensions of transgenerational resilience. We take a deep dive into the psychological, cultural, and societal factors that have shaped the survivors' experiences and the experiences of their children. We explore the intricate interplay between memory, identity, and resilience—a dance of emotions and experiences that define their lives. We engage with the challenges and triumphs that arise when navigating a legacy of trauma, and we learn from the wisdom that emerges from the crucible of adversity.

Through these captivating stories of transgenerational resilience, we hope to inspire, educate, and ignite conversations that foster understanding, empathy, and healing. We extend an invitation to our readers to embark on a transformative journey, one that is illuminated by the radiant power of resilience and the indomitable spirit that resides within the survivors and their descendants.

As we navigate the chapters of "Rebounce," it is incumbent upon us to honor the survivors and their courage. We must recognize the profound intergenerational impact of the Genocide against the Tutsi and celebrate the strength that has been lovingly passed down from one generation to the next. May this book serve not only as a testament to the enduring spirit of resilience but also as a fervent call to action. Let it remind us of our collective responsibility to work tirelessly towards creating a world where such heinous atrocities are never repeated—where the enduring legacy of the survivors is one of resilience, healing, and hope for a brighter future.

Part I: Resilience for resilients

Welcome to "Rebounce: Transgenerational Resilience of Survivors of Genocide against Tutsi." Let us embark on this journey together, as we bear witness to the stories of survival, resilience, and hope.

Rebound is a concept of resilience that holds great significance. It refers to the remarkable ability of individuals or communities to bounce back or recover from adversity. It implies that, even when faced with incredibly difficult or challenging circumstances, people can regain their equilibrium and return to their previous level of functioning, and sometimes even surpass it. The concept of rebound underscores the idea that resilience is not just about surviving in the face of adversity; it's also about thriving and growing in the aftermath of difficult situations.

The various forms that rebound can take depend on the situation and the individuals or communities involved. For example, rebound might involve an individual overcoming a setback or failure and returning to a previous level of success, or even achieving greater success than before. It could also encompass a community's recovery from a disaster or crisis, leading to the rebuilding of stronger and more resilient infrastructure, social systems, and relationships.

Reflecting on my own experiences, I initially hesitated to share my story. I vividly recall a conversation with Dr. Catherine Gilbert, Chair of the Ishami Foundation, where she encouraged me to consider sharing my personal narrative. At the time, I questioned whether I had a story worth sharing. However, I am immensely grateful to her for taking the time to convince me that my story could inspire and uplift others. Over time, I became convinced that sharing my story, along with Aline's, could indeed make a positive impact.

The backdrop against which this discussion unfolds is the devastating Genocide against the Tutsi in Rwanda 1994. This tragic event left the country in ruins, with severe consequences for mental health and social cohesion. The aftermath of the Genocide has been more profound and harrowing than one can ever imagine. We must never forget the innocent victims who perished in that massacre. As someone who has witnessed the journey of survivors on their path to healing, I have come to truly understand what rebound means in the face of such unspeakable tragedy.

We often celebrate the resilience of survivors of the Genocide, but it's important to acknowledge the incredible hardships they faced. Survivors did not simply allow themselves to wither away or remain defeated. They fought relentlessly to attain success. They started businesses, secured jobs, pursued education, formed families, and raised children. This was an extraordinary feat, considering not only the financial losses but also the loss of loved ones – family members, friends, and colleagues. The emotional toll of such losses cannot be underestimated, and it posed a significant obstacle to rebuilding their lives. Many survivors were young, and surviving such a heart-wrenching and merciless massacre left them grappling with severe psychological crises.

Recognizing and honoring the survivors' journey of resilience is of utmost importance. Their ability to rebound from overwhelming adversity has had a lasting impact on their children, the next generation, and Rwandan society as a whole. This enduring legacy of strength and determination has paved the way for transgenerational resilience, leaving an indelible mark on the fabric of our society.

Rebound is a concept that holds profound meaning, emphasizing the capacity of individuals and communities to not only survive adversity but also to thrive and evolve in its aftermath. In this book, I aim to convey the significance of rebound through personal stories, particularly those of survivors of the Genocide against the Tutsi in Rwanda 1994. Their resilience and the enduring impact of their journey on future generations are central themes that resonate throughout this narrative.

Transgenerational resilience in Rwanda

"Imfura igenda nka se" this is the Rwandan proverb that is many years older than me, it say that the son's heroism comes from his father, in Rwanda resilience as one of the sign of braveness is taken to be hereditary, Rwandans have always believed that the father have to teach all the heroism practices to the children and so they pass it to their children too as generation goes, in our culture also talents as well as other clans norms pass in the family for the legacy to be continued. According to the Rwandans proverbs and sayings Rwandans have been resilient people from our old ancestor, they are sayings like "Imfura inshinjagira ishira" which means the brave people have to be patient, all of these such like the others have served to stimulate Rwandans to be brave in tough times and inspire them to aspire heroism in their everyday activities.

As explained by *Dr. Arielle Schwartz "Raising a child is one of the most courageous and vulnerable actions we can take as human beings. Shadows of the past churn and turn towards the light asking us to pay attention to unexpected feelings of ambivalence, comparison, and inadequacy in parenting. Unearthing, and addressing these feelings when they arise unwinds shame and is an essential key to healing our transgenerational attachment legacies"* After the Genocide against the Tutsi as broken as Rwandan society was, parenting and raising children was one of the challenges that Rwandans faced, As transmission of legacy was concerned there was a lot to pay attention on.

Transgenerational resilience among survivors of Genocide against Tutsi have been their ability and community to adapt and recover from the traumatic experiences of the Genocide, and to transmit their resilience to future generations. This resilience can be seen in various forms, including psychological, social, and cultural resilience.

One possible explanation for this resilience is the strong social support networks that many survivors have developed. In many cases, survivors were able to rely on the support of family and friends to help them cope with the trauma of the Genocide. Additionally, survivors may have found strength in their cultural traditions and religious beliefs, which provided them with a sense of purpose and meaning.

Another possible explanation for transgenerational resilience is the importance of education and access to resources. Many survivors have worked hard to rebuild their lives and communities, and have prioritized education and economic development as a means of achieving this goal. By doing so, they have been able to provide their children with greater opportunities for success and resilience.

Finally, the resilience of survivors of Genocide against Tutsi can also be attributed to their ability to create and sustain a sense of collective identity and purpose. By working together towards a common goal, such as promoting justice and reconciliation, survivors have been able to find strength and meaning in their shared experiences and aspirations.

Overall, transgenerational resilience among survivors of Genocide against Tutsi is a complex phenomenon that cannot be fully explained by any one factor. Rather, it is the result of a combination of social, cultural, economic, and political factors that have allowed survivors to adapt and thrive despite the challenges they have faced of unimaginable trauma and loss.

After writing wet under the rainbow, I gave my 5 friends the book to read first, as friendly as they was I didn't expect them to discourage me but what was surprising was how one of them asked "How did you think of all of that?" and I asked her "What?" and then she said "That, my life, your life, our lives." She explained to me that wet under the rainbow which was my book about Trans generational trauma was a true reflection of every youth in this generation. And so yes in Trans generational of legacies, parents transmits their trauma to their children as well as the society knowingly, unknowingly, directly or indirectly. Unresolved trauma of one generation is a legacy that can be passed down to the next generation.

As days passed, colleagues and youth giving me their small testimonies on how I tackled about their life, though their emphasized about the topic of the book which is wet under the rainbow, I always understood transmission of healing and transmission of resilience. I would always understand them telling me how their parents have rebounced, how they are trying to help their family to grow as well as preserving the memory because they knew well that it was their parents strength. This is on the side of the side of children of the survivors against the Tutsi which is different from the side of the children of perpetrators whom a few that we talked with were in the journey of healing and resilience as well.

Writing this book, I wished I would be in the ear of every Genocide against Tutsi 1994 survivors and whisper to them "Rebound" in their everyday struggle to heal, to get over their pain, to raise their children with all the best that they can get, to rebuild their life, to find a new family, to pass their family memories to their friends and family. And I wish also they would understand that she who is telling them learnt how to overcome challenges from them.

As I write, I want every one reading it to learn how to rebound after a certain crisis taking a lesson from Genocide against Tutsi survivors in Rwanda for their selfless resilience, let's talk about the pillars of resilience. This is not only for our elders that passed through a lot in Genocide against Tutsi but also for their children, gran children and grand grand children, you have of rise against your history chains that pulls you down, your family shame or your inherited trauma.

SELF AWARENESS

Self-awareness, the cornerstone of understanding oneself, encompasses a profound grasp of your personality in its entirety, delving deep into the intricacies of your traits, thoughts, beliefs, motivations, and emotions. This introspective capacity not only allows you to fathom your own inner workings but also serves as a powerful lens through which you can interpret and relate to others. It grants you insight into their perceptions of you, your demeanor, and your immediate reactions in their presence.

Reflecting on a personal experience from my youth, I recall the moment when I first encountered a song dedicated to commemorating the victims of the Genocide against the Tutsi 1994. Although I was too young to fully comprehend the historical context, the overwhelming sadness that washed over me was palpable. As a child, I found myself in a state of emotional turmoil, shedding tears without the ability to articulate the source of my distress. I struggled to explain the profound sorrow that had gripped my heart. Moreover, I could not confront or console that helpless, weeping child within me when confronted with the harrowing accounts of the Genocide against the Tutsi.

It wasn't until later in life that I came to appreciate the significance of self-awareness as one of the fundamental pillars of resilience. Self-awareness, I realized, provides the critical framework for understanding our reactions, emotions, and, ultimately, our ability to cope with life's most challenging moments. It is through this profound awareness of self that we can begin to make sense of the inexplicable and find the strength to heal, grow, and contribute positively to the world around us.

SELF CARE

Each person's interpretation of self-care is deeply personal, and the avenues to achieve it are as diverse as the individuals themselves. At its core, self-care encompasses our innate ability as human beings to navigate life's complexities effectively, approaching daily challenges with vitality, resilience, and confidence. It is a proactive endeavor that demands our deliberate engagement and persistent upkeep, irrespective of the hurdles that can transform it into an act of resilience.

Reflecting on the significance of self-care in the context of self-awareness, I am reminded of my mother, a survivor of the Genocide against the Tutsi. She never fully grasped the importance of self-care as a foundational element of resilience. Her belief that both she and her children were "good" was a testament to her strength, but it concealed the unique wounds that every survivor of such a traumatic event carries. These wounds, though different for each individual, demand attention and care. The essence of self-care lies in addressing these wounds in ways that foster physical, mental, and emotional well-being. It equips us to manage the weight of stress and adversity, allowing us to emerge stronger and more resilient in the face of life's challenges.

Part I: Resilience for resilients

MINDFULNESS

Mindfulness, a state of active and undistracted presence in the present moment, represents a profound mental condition that empowers individuals to observe their thoughts and emotions from a standpoint of impartiality, devoid of judgment. It beckons us to fully engage with the unfolding experience of life rather than merely allowing it to slip through our fingers. Have you ever paused to scrutinize your existence and realized that you are, in essence, merely going through the motions? It's a realization that the adversities and trials you confront, much like the challenges in life, contribute to your growth and inner strength. Mindfulness invites you to turn inward, to explore your thoughts and emotions with an open and accepting heart, acknowledging them as they are, without the weight of criticism or denial.

It's a practice that encourages taking deliberate action, stepping towards your goals, and making decisions that align with your values and aspirations. In the gentle dance between awareness and action, mindfulness becomes a guiding light, illuminating the path to a more purposeful and enriched life.

SOCIAL SUPPORT

The support of family, friends, and the wider community stands as an indispensable cornerstone of resilience, providing a robust foundation upon which one can navigate life's challenges. The presence of a support network is not merely a comforting presence but rather a lifeline during times of stress and trauma. It acts as a buffer against the relentless waves of adversity, offering solace and strength when it is needed most. Within this context, consider the significance of a group that not only comprehends your experiences but actively supports you; it plays an integral role in your resilience journey. Take, for instance, the poignant example of AERG (Association des Élèves Rescapés du Génocide contre les Tutsi).

Countless testimonies bear witness to how this organization has been instrumental in helping individuals confront the psychological difficulties stemming from their traumatic past and providing a channel for them to cope with profound loss. As we embark on this journey together through the pages of this book, you will gain deeper insights into how AERG's support played a pivotal role in my own path towards resilience, illustrating the profound impact of collective support on an individual's ability to heal and thrive.

POSITIVE BELIEFS AND ATTITUDES

Sustaining positive beliefs and attitudes emerges as a potent force that can propel individuals forward, maintaining their motivation and unwavering focus, even when confronted with the most formidable of adversities. This positive outlook encompasses a spectrum of attributes, including optimism, self-efficacy, and a profound sense of purpose or meaning in one's life. It is entirely understandable how, in the aftermath of a harrowing experience such as the Genocide against the Tutsi, individuals might find themselves adrift, their sense of life's purpose obscured by the traumatic events they have endured.

In the wake of such profound tragedy, where the future may seem bleak and uncertain, the importance of forging a path toward prosperity becomes even more evident. It begins with rediscovering the purpose of life and cultivating a positive mindset that envisions a brighter future. This transformational journey reflects the indomitable human spirit's capacity not only to survive but also to thrive, anchored in the enduring power of hope and a steadfast belief in the possibility of a better tomorrow.

ADAPTABILITY AND FLEXIBILITY

The capacity to adapt and display flexibility in the face of evolving circumstances is undeniably one of the vital components of resilience. It's an attribute that allows individuals not only to weather the storms of life but also to thrive amid change. This adaptability hinges on the willingness to be receptive to fresh ideas and alternative viewpoints, as well as the readiness to explore innovative problem-solving approaches. From the vantage point of my life experiences within a resilient society, I've gleaned invaluable insights into this facet of resilience. I'm truly delighted to share these insights with you, as they hold the potential to become invaluable tools on your own resilience journey.

Just as a healing journey demands dedication and personal accountability, so does the path to resilience. It is a journey that necessitates effort and perseverance, but I want to emphasize that it is entirely possible. The resilience journey, like life itself, is a dynamic process, and with the right mindset and tools, you can navigate its twists and turns with grace and resilience.

ECONOMIC SECURITY

Economic security and stability stand as a cornerstone of resilience, offering a sturdy foundation upon which individuals and families can build their path to success. The significance of this pillar cannot be overstated, as it equips people with the essential resources and opportunities necessary for not just survival, but thriving. These resources may encompass access to employment opportunities, a financial safety net, and a host of other vital assets. It's crucial to acknowledge that when discussing the pillars of resilience, economic security should never be overlooked or understated. For many, it is an uphill battle to rebuild their lives, particularly when financial crises persist. The process of rebounding from adversity carries its own set of challenges, and one of them is undoubtedly the pursuit of economic security.

This journey often necessitates immense dedication and hard work, as individuals strive to regain their financial footing, and it becomes all the more impactful when coupled with good health. These two aspects, economic security and well-being, intertwine to form a formidable foundation upon which the edifice of resilience can be constructed, demonstrating that true resilience encompasses not only the ability to weather storms but also the strength to rebuild and prosper in their aftermath.

POSITIVE RELATIONSHIPS

Positive relationships represent the very essence of human connection, underlining the profound impact they have on our well-being and the quality of our lives. These connections, forged through mutual support and care, offer some of the most meaningful experiences we can encounter. The bonds we create with fellow human beings form the tapestry of our existence, weaving a rich and colorful narrative of shared joys and sorrows. When we actively cultivate and nurture positive relationships, we open the door to a deeper sense of happiness and fulfillment.

In these connections, we find a wellspring of support, knowing that there are people who genuinely care about our well-being and are there for us when we need them. Simultaneously, we become sources of support, empathy, and understanding for those we cherish. These relationships infuse our lives with vitality and meaning, enhancing our overall health and happiness, and ultimately leading to greater satisfaction with the remarkable journey of life we embark upon.

PURPOSE

Purpose, in its essence, represents the profound realization that our existence extends beyond the confines of our individual selves, as we are part of something greater and interconnected with the world around us. This recognition of belonging and service to a larger purpose plays a transformative role in shaping our mindset and attitude towards both others and the myriad events that unfold in our lives. It's through our sense of purpose that we gain a compass by which to navigate the complexities of existence, providing us with direction, meaning, and a sense of significance.

This purpose can manifest in various forms, ranging from deeply rooted faith and devotion, to the bonds of family, the principles of a political ideology, a commitment to environmental stewardship, or active participation in an organization or social group. Each avenue of purpose carries its unique resonance and significance, contributing to the rich tapestry of human experience. Ultimately, our sense of purpose not only adds depth and dimension to our lives but also serves as a guiding force, imbuing our actions and choices with a greater sense of meaning and fulfillment.

ADAPTATION

Resilience, at its core, signifies not only the capacity to adapt to ever-changing circumstances but also the remarkable ability to rebound and thrive in the face of adversity. It encompasses a dynamic process of growth and transformation that can involve the acquisition of new skills, the adoption of innovative problem-solving strategies, or the discovery of effective coping mechanisms when confronted with life's most challenging situations.

It's essential to recognize that the timeline for adaptation and resilience varies for each individual. Sometimes, the ability to bounce back may emerge swiftly in response to a specific problem, while at other times, it may evolve gradually over time. The key takeaway, however, is that regardless of when or how it occurs, the act of bouncing back is what truly matters. It underscores the inherent human capacity to not only survive but also to thrive, emerging from adversity with newfound strength, wisdom, and resilience.

COPING

Coping refers to the strategies and behaviors that individuals use to manage stress and overcome challenges. Effective coping strategies may include seeking social support, practicing relaxation techniques, or engaging in physical exercise.

All this is advisable as I wrote this book to learn from survivor's resilience to build our own, you can find your own way of coping with the trauma or even trans-generational trauma to have transgenerational resilience by learning how you family, guardians or community coped to bounce back.

Part I: Resilience for resilients

STRENGTHS-BASED APPROACH

Resilience is often viewed as a strengths-based approach, which focuses on identifying and building upon the strengths and resources that individuals and communities already possess. This may involve fostering positive beliefs and attitudes, cultivating social connections, and developing skills and knowledge to help you to bounce back.

PROTECTIVE FACTORS

Resilience is often seen as a dynamic interaction between risk and protective factors. Risk factors may include things like poverty, trauma, or social isolation, while protective factors may include social support, positive coping strategies, and a sense of purpose or meaning. After a certain traumatic event, it's not an end of other life difficulties that may pull you down, we have to have risk protective factors which is a risks stand by solutions which can help us to cop to other life difficulties more easily.

Overall, pillars and concepts of resilience emphasizes the importance of adaptability, coping, and strengths-based approaches in the face of adversity and challenges, and highlights the dynamic interaction between risk and protective factors as well as having some after difficulties mechanism to help you to bounce back.

CHAPTER 2: The Resilient Mindset: Cognitive Tools for Overcoming Challenges

Resilience is a multifaceted concept often depicted through various "Rs," each shedding light on different facets and attributes of this remarkable human quality. While different perspectives and sources may introduce variations, several commonly mentioned "Rs" provide a comprehensive understanding of resilience. The first among them is resourcefulness, a fundamental aspect that underscores the ability to not only identify but also efficiently harness available resources, whether they are internal strengths or external support systems. Resourcefulness empowers individuals to navigate challenges and adversity with creativity and adaptability, making the most of what's at hand to facilitate adaptation and recovery. It's a quality that serves as a cornerstone in the resilience toolkit, enabling individuals to confront life's complexities with a sense of confidence and purpose.

Resourcefulness encompasses several key aspects:
Identifying Resources: Resourcefulness involves recognizing the various resources that can be accessed or utilized in a given situation. These resources can include personal strengths, skills, knowledge, social support networks, financial means, technology, information, and other tangible or intangible assets.

Problem-Solving: Resourcefulness requires a problem-solving mindset, where individuals actively seek solutions and alternatives to address the challenges they face. It involves thinking outside the box, being innovative, and exploring different approaches to overcome obstacles.

Adaptability: Being resourceful means being adaptable and flexible in the face of changing circumstances. It involves adjusting strategies and utilizing different resources as the situation demands, while staying focused on the goal of resilience and recovery.

Part I: Resilience for resilients

Making the Most of Limited Resources: Resourcefulness also involves optimizing the use of limited resources. It means finding ways to maximize the effectiveness and efficiency of available resources, making strategic choices, and prioritizing based on the importance and impact of each resource.

Seeking Support and Collaboration: Resourcefulness includes recognizing when to seek help and support from others. It means leveraging social networks, reaching out to experts or mentors, and collaborating with others who may have valuable knowledge or resources that can contribute to resilience.

Reflection: Involves the practice of introspection and self-assessment to understand one's emotions, thoughts, and reactions in the face of adversity. Reflection helps in learning from experiences and developing strategies for coping and bouncing back.

- Self-Awareness: Reflection begins with self-awareness, which involves being attuned to one's emotions, thoughts, strengths, weaknesses, and patterns of behavior. It entails recognizing how these factors influence one's responses to challenging situations.
- Learning from Experience: Reflection involves looking back on past experiences and extracting lessons or insights from them. It entails examining both successes and failures to identify what worked well and what could be improved.
- Emotional Processing: When engaging in reflection, individuals examine their emotional reactions to adversity. They strive to understand the underlying emotions, triggers, and patterns, which can help them better manage their emotions and respond more effectively in the future.
- Identifying Strengths and Areas for Growth: Reflection allows individuals to identify their personal strengths and resources that helped them navigate difficult situations. It also helps identify areas for growth and areas where additional support or development may be beneficial.

- Adjusting Perspectives: Reflection enables individuals to evaluate their perspectives and beliefs about themselves, others, and the world. It can involve challenging negative or limiting beliefs and adopting more adaptive and resilient perspectives.
- Setting Goals and Strategies: Reflection contributes to setting goals and developing strategies for personal growth and resilience. It helps individuals identify areas they want to work on, set realistic goals, and devise action plans to achieve those goals.
- Continuous Learning and Improvement: Reflection is an ongoing process that promotes continuous learning and improvement. It encourages individuals to apply the insights gained from reflection to future challenges and develop adaptive strategies to enhance resilience.

Relationships: Highlighting the importance of social connections, relationships contribute to resilience. Having a supportive network of family, friends, or colleagues can provide emotional support, practical assistance, and a sense of belonging during difficult times.

- Self-Awareness: Reflection begins with self-awareness, which involves being attuned to one's emotions, thoughts, strengths, weaknesses, and patterns of behavior. It entails recognizing how these factors influence one's responses to challenging situations.
- Learning from Experience: Reflection involves looking back on past experiences and extracting lessons or insights from them. It entails examining both successes and failures to identify what worked well and what could be improved.
- Emotional Processing: When engaging in reflection, individuals examine their emotional reactions to adversity. They strive to understand the underlying emotions, triggers, and patterns, which can help them better manage their emotions and respond more effectively in the future.
- Identifying Strengths and Areas for Growth: Reflection allows individuals to identify their personal strengths and resources that helped them navigate difficult situations. It also helps identify areas

for growth and areas where additional support or development may be beneficial.

- Adjusting Perspectives: Reflection enables individuals to evaluate their perspectives and beliefs about themselves, others, and the world. It can involve challenging negative or limiting beliefs and adopting more adaptive and resilient perspectives.
- Setting Goals and Strategies: Reflection contributes to setting goals and developing strategies for personal growth and resilience. It helps individuals identify areas they want to work on, set realistic goals, and devise action plans to achieve those goals.
- Continuous Learning and Improvement: Reflection is an ongoing process that promotes continuous learning and improvement. It encourages individuals to apply the insights gained from reflection to future challenges and develop adaptive strategies to enhance resilience.
- Responsibility: Refers to taking ownership of one's actions, emotions, and responses. Accepting personal responsibility empowers individuals to take proactive steps in addressing challenges and overcoming adversity.
- Self-Awareness: Reflection begins with self-awareness, which involves being attuned to one's emotions, thoughts, strengths, weaknesses, and patterns of behavior. It entails recognizing how these factors influence one's responses to challenging situations.
- Learning from Experience: Reflection involves looking back on past experiences and extracting lessons or insights from them. It entails examining both successes and failures to identify what worked well and what could be improved.
- Emotional Processing: When engaging in reflection, individuals examine their emotional reactions to adversity. They strive to understand the underlying emotions, triggers, and patterns, which can help them better manage their emotions and respond more effectively in the future.
- Identifying Strengths and Areas for Growth: Reflection allows individuals to identify their personal strengths and resources that helped them navigate difficult situations. It also helps identify areas

for growth and areas where additional support or development may be beneficial.

- Adjusting Perspectives: Reflection enables individuals to evaluate their perspectives and beliefs about themselves, others, and the world. It can involve challenging negative or limiting beliefs and adopting more adaptive and resilient perspectives.
- Setting Goals and Strategies: Reflection contributes to setting goals and developing strategies for personal growth and resilience. It helps individuals identify areas they want to work on, set realistic goals, and devise action plans to achieve those goals.
- Continuous Learning and Improvement: Reflection is an ongoing process that promotes continuous learning and improvement. It encourages individuals to apply the insights gained from reflection to future challenges and develop adaptive strategies to enhance resilience.

Resolve: Involves the determination and perseverance to face difficulties head-on, maintain a positive mindset, and persistently work towards goals despite setbacks or obstacles.

Determination: Resolve involves a strong sense of determination and perseverance. It is the unwavering commitment to overcome difficulties and pursue goals, despite setbacks or obstacles that may arise.

Persistence: Resilient individuals demonstrate persistence by staying engaged in the face of adversity. They maintain their efforts, continually taking steps forward, and refuse to give up or be discouraged by setbacks.

- Focus: Resolve entails maintaining focus and concentration on the desired outcomes and goals, despite distractions or challenges. Resilient individuals keep their attention directed toward what they want to achieve, guiding their actions and decisions accordingly.
- Positive Mindset: Resolve is often accompanied by a positive mindset. Resilient individuals maintain an optimistic outlook and believe in their ability to overcome challenges. They approach obstacles as opportunities for growth and see setbacks as temporary hurdles.

Part I: Resilience for resilients

- Inner Strength: Resolve represents inner strength—the resilience and mental toughness that individuals draw upon in challenging times. It is the internal resilience that enables them to face adversity head-on and persevere.
- Goal Orientation: Resolve is closely tied to goal orientation. Resilient individuals have a clear sense of purpose and direction, setting meaningful goals and working steadfastly toward achieving them.
- Adaptability: Resolve is adaptable. Resilient individuals are willing to adjust their plans and strategies when necessary, without compromising their commitment to their ultimate objectives.
- Courage: Resolve requires courage—the willingness to take risks and step out of one's comfort zone. Resilient individuals are not afraid to face difficult situations and make bold decisions in pursuit of their goals.
- Realistic optimism: Combines the understanding of reality and challenges with an optimistic outlook. It involves acknowledging the difficulties while maintaining a positive belief in one's ability to overcome them.
- Determination: Resolve involves a strong sense of determination and perseverance. It is the unwavering commitment to overcome difficulties and pursue goals, despite setbacks or obstacles that may arise.
- Persistence: Resilient individuals demonstrate persistence by staying engaged in the face of adversity. They maintain their efforts, continually taking steps forward, and refuse to give up or be discouraged by setbacks.
- Focus: Resolve entails maintaining focus and concentration on the desired outcomes and goals, despite distractions or challenges. Resilient individuals keep their attention directed toward what they want to achieve, guiding their actions and decisions accordingly.
- Positive Mindset: Resolve is often accompanied by a positive mindset. Resilient individuals maintain an optimistic outlook and believe in their ability to overcome challenges. They approach obstacles as opportunities for growth and see setbacks as temporary hurdles.
- Inner Strength: Resolve represents inner strength—the resilience and mental toughness that individuals draw upon in challenging times. It is

the internal resilience that enables them to face adversity head-on and persevere.

- Goal Orientation: Resolve is closely tied to goal orientation. Resilient individuals have a clear sense of purpose and direction, setting meaningful goals and working steadfastly toward achieving them.
- Adaptability: Resolve is adaptable. Resilient individuals are willing to adjust their plans and strategies when necessary, without compromising their commitment to their ultimate objectives.
- Courage: Resolve requires courage—the willingness to take risks and step out of one's comfort zone. Resilient individuals are not afraid to face difficult situations and make bold decisions in pursuit of their goals.

Self-care: Emphasizes the importance of self-preservation and maintaining well-being. Practicing self-care involves taking care of physical, emotional, and mental health, engaging in activities that promote relaxation and rejuvenation.

- Growth and Learning: Risk-taking is essential for personal and professional growth. By taking risks, individuals expose themselves to new experiences, challenges, and opportunities for learning. It helps expand their comfort zones, develop new skills, and build resilience by adapting to different circumstances.
- Adaptability: Resilient individuals are open to change and willing to take risks to adapt to new situations. They understand that the world is constantly evolving, and being adaptable is crucial for thriving in dynamic environments. They embrace challenges and view them as opportunities for growth rather than threats.
- Overcoming Fear: Risk-taking in resilience requires individuals to overcome their fears and anxieties. It involves confronting the unknown, accepting the possibility of failure, and pushing through discomfort. By confronting their fears, resilient individuals build courage and develop a stronger capacity to face future challenges.
- Decision-Making: Risk-taking involves making informed decisions that consider potential risks and rewards. Resilient individuals assess the potential consequences of their actions, weigh the potential benefits

against the potential downsides, and make calculated choices. They also learn from past experiences to improve their decision-making process.

- Innovation and Creativity: Risk-taking often leads to innovation and creativity. By exploring uncharted territories and taking unconventional paths, individuals can discover new solutions and approaches. Resilient individuals embrace a mindset of experimentation and are willing to challenge the status quo to find innovative ways of overcoming obstacles.
- Managing Risks: While risk-taking is important, it's crucial to manage and mitigate risks effectively. Resilient individuals assess risks, plan and prepare accordingly, and take necessary precautions to minimize potential negative outcomes. They balance the potential benefits of risk-taking with the need for risk management.

Risk-taking: Implies a willingness to step out of one's comfort zone and embrace calculated risks. Taking risks can lead to new opportunities, personal growth, and enhanced resilience.

Growth and Learning: Risk-taking is essential for personal and professional growth. By taking risks, individuals expose themselves to new experiences, challenges, and opportunities for learning. It helps expand their comfort zones, develop new skills, and build resilience by adapting to different circumstances.

Adaptability: Resilient individuals are open to change and willing to take risks to adapt to new situations. They understand that the world is constantly evolving, and being adaptable is crucial for thriving in dynamic environments. They embrace challenges and view them as opportunities for growth rather than threats.

Overcoming Fear: Risk-taking in resilience requires individuals to overcome their fears and anxieties. It involves confronting the unknown, accepting the possibility of failure, and pushing through discomfort. By confronting their fears, resilient individuals build courage and develop a stronger capacity to face future challenges.

Decision-Making: Risk-taking involves making informed decisions that consider potential risks and rewards. Resilient individuals assess the potential consequences of their actions, weigh the potential benefits against the potential downsides, and make calculated choices. They also learn from past experiences to improve their decision-making process.

Innovation and Creativity: Risk-taking often leads to innovation and creativity. By exploring uncharted territories and taking unconventional paths, individuals can discover new solutions and approaches. Resilient individuals embrace a mindset of experimentation and are willing to challenge the status quo to find innovative ways of overcoming obstacles.

Managing Risks: While risk-taking is important, it's crucial to manage and mitigate risks effectively. Resilient individuals assess risks, plan and prepare accordingly, and take necessary precautions to minimize potential negative outcomes. They balance the potential benefits of risk-taking with the need for risk management.

Resourcing: Refers to building and leveraging external support systems, such as mentors, coaches, or therapists. Seeking guidance from experts and utilizing available resources can aid in developing resilience.

- Determination: Resolve involves a strong sense of determination and perseverance. It is the unwavering commitment to overcome difficulties and pursue goals, despite setbacks or obstacles that may arise.
- Persistence: Resilient individuals demonstrate persistence by staying engaged in the face of adversity. They maintain their efforts, continually taking steps forward, and refuse to give up or be discouraged by setbacks.
- Focus: Resolve entails maintaining focus and concentration on the desired outcomes and goals, despite distractions or challenges. Resilient individuals keep their attention directed toward what they want to achieve, guiding their actions and decisions accordingly.
- Positive Mindset: Resolve is often accompanied by a positive mindset. Resilient individuals maintain an optimistic outlook and believe in

their ability to overcome challenges. They approach obstacles as opportunities for growth and see setbacks as temporary hurdles.

- Inner Strength: Resolve represents inner strength—the resilience and mental toughness that individuals draw upon in challenging times. It is the internal resilience that enables them to face adversity head-on and persevere.
- Goal Orientation: Resolve is closely tied to goal orientation. Resilient individuals have a clear sense of purpose and direction, setting meaningful goals and working steadfastly toward achieving them.
- Adaptability: Resolve is adaptable. Resilient individuals are willing to adjust their plans and strategies when necessary, without compromising their commitment to their ultimate objectives.
- Courage: Resolve requires courage—the willingness to take risks and step out of one's comfort zone. Resilient individuals are not afraid to face difficult situations and make bold decisions in pursuit of their goals.

RECOGNISE "recognize" refers to the ability to identify and acknowledge one's emotions, strengths, weaknesses, and the situations or factors that may impact resilience. It involves being aware of one's internal experiences and external circumstances in order to effectively navigate challenges and foster personal growth. Here are some key points about recognition in resilience:

Self-Awareness: Recognition begins with self-awareness. It involves developing an understanding of one's thoughts, emotions, and behaviors. By being attuned to one's internal experiences, individuals can gain insight into their strengths, areas for improvement, and how they typically respond to stress or adversity.

Emotion Recognition: Resilience requires recognizing and managing emotions effectively. This involves being aware of one's emotions in the moment, understanding their underlying causes, and responding to them in a healthy and adaptive manner. Emotion recognition allows individuals to regulate their emotions and make informed decisions instead of being overwhelmed or reactive.

Part I: Resilience for resilients

Strengths and Weaknesses: Recognizing one's strengths and weaknesses is important for resilience. Understanding personal strengths helps individuals leverage their abilities and resources to overcome challenges. Similarly, recognizing weaknesses or areas for improvement allows individuals to seek support, develop new skills, or implement strategies to enhance their resilience.

External Factors: Recognition also extends to external factors that may impact resilience. This includes being aware of the various stressors, triggers, or obstacles in one's environment. By recognizing these external factors, individuals can proactively plan and adapt their responses to effectively navigate challenges and minimize their impact on well-being.

Feedback and Learning: Recognition involves being open to feedback and embracing a learning mindset. It entails seeking constructive feedback from trusted sources, reflecting on past experiences, and recognizing areas for growth. By being receptive to feedback, individuals can continuously learn, adapt, and strengthen their resilience.

Resilience in Others: Recognition also encompasses recognizing resilience in others. By observing and acknowledging resilience in individuals who have faced adversity or demonstrated strength, individuals can learn from their experiences and gain inspiration. Recognizing resilience in others can also foster a sense of connection and support within communities or social networks.

Respond: refers to the actions and behaviors individuals engage in when faced with adversity or challenging situations. It encompasses the ability to react and adapt in a constructive and effective manner, with the goal of overcoming obstacles and maintaining well-being. The way individuals respond to adversity plays a crucial role in building and demonstrating resilience.

- Awareness and Acknowledgment: Responding to adversity begins with recognizing and acknowledging the challenges or setbacks. It involves being aware of the situation, understanding its impact, and accepting its presence. By acknowledging the adversity, individuals can start formulating a response.

Part I: Resilience for resilients

- Emotional Regulation: Resilient responses involve managing and regulating emotions in the face of adversity. This includes recognizing and accepting the emotions that arise, such as frustration, sadness, or anger, and finding healthy ways to process and cope with them. Emotional regulation allows individuals to maintain a clear and focused mindset while navigating challenges.
- This includes engaging in problem-solving, brainstorming ideas, and considering potential strategies or options to overcome obstacles. Resilient individuals take a proactive approach, focusing on finding practical solutions rather than dwelling on the problem itself.
- Flexibility and Adaptability: Responding resiliently requires being flexible and adaptable in the face of changing circumstances. Resilient individuals recognize that not all situations can be controlled, and they adjust their plans, expectations, and approaches as needed. They are open to new ideas and willing to pivot when necessary, allowing them to navigate unforeseen challenges with greater ease.
- Seeking Support: Resilience involves recognizing the importance of social support and seeking help when needed. Resilient individuals reach out to trusted friends, family members, mentors, or professionals for guidance, advice, and emotional support. Seeking support not only provides individuals with a different perspective but also helps alleviate feelings of isolation and promotes resilience through connectedness.
- Learning and Growth: Responding resiliently includes embracing challenges as opportunities for learning and personal growth. Resilient individuals reflect on their experiences, extract lessons, and integrate newfound knowledge into their responses. They use setbacks as stepping stones for improvement and view failures as valuable learning experiences.
- Maintaining Optimism: Resilient responses often involve maintaining an optimistic outlook and focusing on possibilities rather than dwelling on limitations. This positive mindset allows individuals to approach challenges with hope, resilience, and a belief in their ability to overcome adversity.

Part I: Resilience for resilients

Reframe: refers to the process of shifting perspectives, changing interpretations, or altering the meaning assigned to a situation or event. It involves looking at challenges or setbacks from a different angle in order to find more positive, empowering, or adaptive interpretations. Reframing is a cognitive strategy that can help individuals build resilience by fostering a more constructive and optimistic outlook.

- Shifting Perspectives: Reframing involves intentionally changing the way we view a situation. It requires recognizing that there are different ways to interpret events and consciously choosing to adopt a more helpful or positive perspective. By shifting perspectives, individuals can find new insights, possibilities, or lessons within the challenges they face.

- Positive Reframing: One common form of reframing in resilience is positive reframing. This involves intentionally focusing on the positive aspects or potential benefits of a situation. It doesn't mean ignoring or denying the difficulties, but rather emphasizing the opportunities for growth, learning, or personal development that can arise from adversity.

- Cognitive Flexibility: Reframing requires cognitive flexibility, which is the ability to adapt and shift mental frameworks or interpretations. Resilient individuals are able to consider multiple perspectives, challenge negative or limiting beliefs, and find alternative explanations or meanings for the events they encounter. Cognitive flexibility enables individuals to find adaptive solutions and adapt their responses to different situations.

- Challenging Negative Thoughts: Reframing involves challenging negative thoughts or assumptions that may contribute to a pessimistic or defeatist mindset. Resilient individuals actively question their negative self-talk, identify cognitive distortions (such as catastrophizing or overgeneralization), and replace them with more realistic or empowering thoughts. By reframing negative thinking patterns, individuals can cultivate a more resilient and positive mindset.

- Finding Silver Linings: Reframing also involves identifying the silver linings or positive aspects within challenging situations. This can involve focusing on personal strengths that are strengthened through adversity, recognizing the support and connections that emerge during difficult times, or finding unexpected opportunities for personal or professional growth.

- Empowering Narratives: Reframing includes creating empowering narratives or stories about one's experiences. It involves consciously choosing interpretations that foster a sense of personal agency, resilience, and optimism. By reframing a situation as a valuable learning experience or a stepping stone toward personal growth, individuals can reframe their narratives in a way that supports their resilience.
- Cultivating Resilient Mindsets: Reframing is a fundamental tool for cultivating resilient mindsets. It helps individuals develop a more optimistic and empowered outlook, focusing on possibilities rather than limitations. By reframing challenges as opportunities for growth and finding alternative interpretations, individuals can build resilience and navigate adversity with greater strength and adaptability.

Role model: A role model in resilience refers to someone who embodies and exemplifies the characteristics and behaviors associated with resilience. They serve as an example and source of inspiration for others in building and maintaining their own resilience. Role models in resilience demonstrate strength, perseverance, adaptability, and positive coping strategies in the face of adversity, and their actions and attitudes can inspire others to cultivate similar qualities.

- Modeling Resilient Behaviors: Role models in resilience demonstrate behaviors and actions that promote resilience. They exhibit positive coping strategies, problem-solving skills, emotional regulation, and adaptive responses to challenges. By observing and learning from their behaviors, individuals can gain insight into effective ways of navigating difficulties and develop their own resilience.
- Inspiring Hope and Optimism: Role models in resilience inspire hope and optimism through their actions and attitudes. They showcase a belief in the possibility of overcoming adversity and convey a sense of confidence in their ability to bounce back. This optimism can be contagious and encourage others to adopt a more positive outlook and develop resilience in the face of their own challenges.

Part I: Resilience for resilients

- Sharing Personal Stories: Role models in resilience often share their personal stories of overcoming obstacles and setbacks. By openly discussing their experiences, they provide others with a sense of connection and perspective. Hearing about the challenges they faced, the strategies they employed, and the lessons they learned can inspire and motivate individuals to persevere in their own journeys toward resilience.
- Providing Guidance and Support: Role models in resilience may actively provide guidance and support to others seeking to build their resilience. They offer advice, mentorship, or a listening ear to individuals who are facing challenges. This guidance can help individuals gain new insights, develop coping strategies, and feel supported in their own resilience-building efforts.
- Demonstrating Vulnerability and Growth: Resilient role models are not invulnerable to setbacks or difficulties. They openly acknowledge their vulnerabilities and the challenges they have faced. By demonstrating vulnerability and sharing their own growth process, they normalize the ups and downs of resilience and show that it is a journey of continuous learning and development.
- Fostering Belief in Self: Role models in resilience help foster a belief in one's own ability to overcome adversity. By witnessing someone else's resilience in action, individuals can develop a sense of self-efficacy and the confidence that they too can navigate challenges and bounce back. Role models inspire individuals to trust in their own strengths and capabilities.
- Encouraging Resilient Relationships: Resilient role models can inspire individuals to seek and foster resilient relationships. By observing the support and connections role models have, individuals can recognize the importance of social support and develop their own networks of supportive relationships. Role models demonstrate the value of seeking help, leaning on others during difficult times, and providing support to others in need.

It's important to note that the "Rs" of resilience can vary and additional factors may be included in different contexts. The list provided here offers

Part I: Resilience for resilients

a comprehensive overview of commonly referenced Rs associated with resilience.

Six Cs of Resilience

Commonly referenced framework is the "Six Cs of Resilience," which includes the following elements:

Competence: Refers to having a sense of self-efficacy and the skills, knowledge, and abilities to cope with challenges effectively.

- Problem-Solving Skills: Competence involves the ability to identify problems, analyze them, and generate effective solutions. Resilient individuals are skilled at breaking down complex challenges into manageable tasks and developing strategies to overcome them.
- Emotional Regulation: Competence includes the capacity to recognize, understand, and manage one's emotions in response to stress and adversity. Resilient individuals are able to regulate their emotions, stay calm under pressure, and make rational decisions even in difficult situations.
- Adaptability: Competence involves being flexible and adaptable in the face of change and uncertainty. Resilient individuals can adjust their strategies, plans, and perspectives to navigate shifting circumstances effectively.
- Self-Efficacy: Competence includes a sense of self-efficacy, which is the belief in one's own ability to successfully handle challenges and achieve desired outcomes. Resilient individuals have confidence in their skills, knowledge, and capacities, which enhances their resilience.
- Resourcefulness: Competence involves the ability to identify and utilize available resources to cope with adversity. Resilient individuals are resourceful and can leverage their own strengths and external support systems to navigate challenges effectively.
- Learning and Growth Orientation: Competence includes a mindset of continuous learning and growth. Resilient individuals see setbacks and failures as opportunities for personal development and learning. They

actively seek lessons and insights from difficult experiences, which contributes to their ongoing resilience.

Confidence: Involves having a positive belief in one's own abilities and strengths to overcome difficulties and bounce back from setbacks.

- Belief in Self: Confidence involves having a positive and realistic belief in one's own capabilities. Resilient individuals have a sense of self-assurance and trust in their ability to handle difficulties and navigate through adversity.
- Optimism and Positive Outlook: Confidence includes maintaining an optimistic and positive outlook, even in the face of challenges. Resilient individuals believe that they can overcome setbacks and view them as temporary obstacles rather than insurmountable barriers.
- Self-Worth and Self-Value: Confidence encompasses a sense of self-worth and self-value. Resilient individuals recognize their own inherent worth and value, which helps them maintain a positive self-image even when faced with adversity.
- Resilient Mindset: Confidence contributes to developing a resilient mindset, where individuals have the belief that they can adapt, learn, and grow from adversity. This mindset allows them to approach challenges with a sense of determination and perseverance.
- Persistence and Tenacity: Confidence involves the willingness to persist and remain tenacious in the face of obstacles. Resilient individuals have the confidence to keep trying, even when faced with setbacks or failures, and maintain their motivation to overcome challenges.
- Self-Advocacy: Confidence includes the ability to advocate for oneself and assert one's needs and boundaries. Resilient individuals have the confidence to seek help and support when needed, as well as to communicate effectively in challenging situations.
- Connection: Emphasizes the importance of supportive relationships and social connections, which provide emotional support, guidance, and resources during times of adversity.
- Social Support: Connection involves having access to a network of supportive relationships, including family, friends, colleagues,

mentors, or community members. Resilient individuals have people they can rely on for emotional support, encouragement, and practical assistance during challenging times.

- Trust and Communication: Connection is built on trust and effective communication. Resilient individuals have open and honest communication with their support network, allowing them to express their needs, concerns, and emotions. They feel comfortable seeking help and sharing their experiences with trusted individuals.
- Sense of Belonging: Connection includes a sense of belonging and being a part of a larger community or group. Resilient individuals have a support system that helps them feel connected, valued, and included. This sense of belonging contributes to their overall well-being and resilience.
- Reciprocity: Connection involves a two-way exchange of support and care. Resilient individuals not only receive support from others but also offer support to their network when needed. This reciprocal relationship strengthens connections and fosters resilience in both individuals.
- Diverse Relationships: Connection encompasses a variety of relationships, including both close personal connections and broader community connections. Resilient individuals have a diverse network that provides different perspectives, resources, and sources of support.
- Resilient Communities: Connection extends beyond individual relationships to include the broader community or social context. Resilient individuals are part of communities that prioritize support, collaboration, and collective resilience. These communities provide a supportive environment and resources that contribute to individual resilience.

Character: Relates to the development of positive personal qualities such as perseverance, integrity, and a sense of purpose, which contribute to resilience.

- Integrity: Character involves having a strong sense of integrity and ethical principles. Resilient individuals have a moral compass that guides their actions and decision-making, even in difficult circumstances. They uphold values such as honesty, fairness, and responsibility.

- Perseverance: Character includes the ability to persevere and persist in the face of obstacles and setbacks. Resilient individuals demonstrate determination, grit, and a willingness to continue working towards their goals, even when faced with adversity.
- Courage: Character encompasses the courage to face challenges, take risks, and step out of one's comfort zone. Resilient individuals show bravery and are willing to confront difficult situations or make necessary changes, despite the fear or uncertainty involved.
- Resilient Mindset: Character involves cultivating a resilient mindset, characterized by optimism, hope, and a belief in one's ability to adapt and recover. Resilient individuals maintain a positive outlook, view setbacks as temporary, and see failures as learning opportunities.
- Empathy and Compassion: Character includes the capacity for empathy and compassion towards oneself and others. Resilient individuals are able to understand and relate to the experiences and emotions of others, as well as extend kindness and support to themselves and those around them.

Sense of Purpose: Character encompasses a sense of purpose and meaning in life. Resilient individuals have a clear understanding of their values, goals, and what gives their life significance. This sense of purpose provides motivation and direction, even in challenging times.

- Self-Reflection and Growth: Character involves the willingness to engage in self-reflection and personal growth. Resilient individuals actively seek self-improvement, learn from their experiences, and continually work on developing their character strengths.

Contribution: Refers to the act of giving back or making a positive difference in the lives of others, which can enhance resilience by fostering a sense of purpose and meaning.

- Helping Others: Contribution involves engaging in acts of kindness, support, and assistance to others. Resilient individuals actively look for opportunities to help and uplift those around them, whether through small acts of kindness or more significant acts of service.

- Empowering Others: Contribution includes empowering others to develop their own resilience. Resilient individuals share knowledge, resources, and skills to help others build their capacity to navigate challenges and bounce back from setbacks.
- Mentoring and Role Modeling: Contribution involves serving as a mentor or role model for others, particularly those who may be facing adversity or in need of guidance. Resilient individuals provide support, encouragement, and guidance to inspire and motivate others to develop their resilience.
- Social Engagement: Contribution encompasses active participation and engagement in the community. Resilient individuals actively contribute to community initiatives, volunteering, and collaborating with others to address social issues and create positive change.
- Making a Difference: Contribution involves working towards making a positive impact on a larger scale. Resilient individuals strive to leave a meaningful legacy by contributing their skills, expertise, and resources to address societal challenges or promote positive change in their chosen fields or areas of interest.
- Sense of Purpose and Meaning: Contribution provides a sense of purpose and meaning in life. Resilient individuals find fulfillment and satisfaction in making a positive difference in the lives of others. This sense of purpose strengthens their own resilience and motivates them to continue contributing.
- Coping: Involves the ability to employ effective coping strategies and adaptive responses to stress, adversity, and trauma.
- Adaptive Coping Strategies: Coping involves the use of adaptive strategies to effectively deal with stress and adversity. Resilient individuals employ healthy and constructive coping mechanisms, such as problem-solving, seeking social support, practicing self-care, and engaging in relaxation techniques.
- Emotional Regulation: Coping includes the ability to manage and regulate one's emotions in response to challenges. Resilient individuals develop emotional awareness and utilize strategies to regulate their emotions, such as mindfulness, deep breathing, or engaging in activities that bring joy and relaxation.

- Stress Management: Coping involves developing effective stress management techniques to reduce the negative impact of stress on well-being. Resilient individuals engage in activities such as exercise, meditation, hobbies, or engaging in activities that promote relaxation and stress reduction.
- Flexibility and Adaptability: Coping encompasses the ability to adapt and adjust to new circumstances and changes. Resilient individuals are flexible in their thinking and behavior, able to adjust their coping strategies and approaches based on the demands of the situation.
- Seeking Support: Coping includes recognizing the importance of seeking and utilizing social support when facing challenges. Resilient individuals reach out to trusted individuals, such as friends, family, or mental health professionals, to seek guidance, validation, and assistance during difficult times.
- Cognitive Restructuring: Coping involves reframing and shifting one's perspective and thoughts about challenges. Resilient individuals engage in cognitive restructuring, challenging negative or unhelpful thoughts and replacing them with more positive and realistic ones, which can contribute to a more resilient mindset.
- Self-Care: Coping includes prioritizing self-care activities that promote well-being and resilience. Resilient individuals engage in practices such as adequate sleep, healthy nutrition, exercise, leisure activities, and engaging in activities that bring joy and fulfillment.

Challenge: The "C" represents the ability to perceive and approach difficult situations as challenges rather than insurmountable obstacles. Resilient individuals view adversity as an opportunity for growth, learning, and development. They have a mindset that embraces challenges, remains open to new experiences, and sees setbacks as temporary and surmountable.

- Growth Mindset: Challenge involves adopting a growth mindset, which is the belief that abilities and intelligence can be developed through effort, practice, and learning. Resilient individuals see challenges as a chance to improve their skills, expand their knowledge, and develop new strengths.

- Positive Reframing: Challenge includes the ability to reframe or re-interpret difficult situations in a positive light. Resilient individuals focus on the potential benefits, opportunities, or lessons that can emerge from facing and overcoming challenges. They seek to find meaning and purpose in adversity.
- Problem-Solving: Challenge encompasses the capacity to approach problems and obstacles with a solution-oriented mindset. Resilient individuals engage in effective problem-solving strategies, breaking down challenges into manageable steps and seeking creative solutions.
- Adaptability: Challenge involves being adaptable and flexible in the face of change or unexpected circumstances. Resilient individuals embrace uncertainty and are open to adjusting their plans, strategies, or approaches to meet the demands of challenging situations.
- Learning Orientation: Challenge includes a willingness to learn from experiences, including failures and setbacks. Resilient individuals view challenges as learning opportunities and use them as a chance to gain new insights, acquire new skills, and refine their approaches.
- Embracing Discomfort: Challenge encompasses being comfortable with discomfort and stepping outside of one's comfort zone. Resilient individuals recognize that growth and resilience often come from facing and navigating challenging and unfamiliar situations.

Control: The second "C" refers to having a sense of control over one's own actions, choices, and responses in the face of adversity. Resilient individuals recognize that they have some influence over their circumstances, even if they cannot control everything. They focus on what is within their control, such as their attitude, efforts, and decision-making, rather than fixating on factors beyond their control.

- Internal Locus of Control: Control encompasses having an internal locus of control, which means believing that one has the power to influence and shape outcomes through their own actions and decisions. Resilient individuals believe that they have some control over their lives, even if they cannot control every external factor.
- Adaptive Coping Strategies: Control involves utilizing adaptive coping strategies to manage and navigate through difficult situations.

Resilient individuals identify healthy and constructive ways to cope with stress, such as problem-solving, seeking support, practicing self-care, and engaging in relaxation techniques.

- Emotional Regulation: Control includes the ability to regulate and manage one's own emotions in response to challenging circumstances. Resilient individuals develop emotional awareness and employ strategies to cope with and control their emotional reactions, enabling them to respond more effectively to adversity.
- Acceptance of What Cannot be Controlled: Control also involves accepting and letting go of factors that are beyond one's control. Resilient individuals recognize that there are certain aspects of a situation that cannot be changed and focus instead on adapting their responses and attitudes to what is within their control.
- Focus on Influence: Control encompasses focusing on areas where one can exert influence and make a difference. Resilient individuals identify aspects of a situation where they can have an impact and direct their energy towards those areas, rather than dwelling on what they cannot control.
- Proactive Approach: Control involves taking a proactive approach to problem-solving and decision-making. Resilient individuals actively seek solutions, make choices based on their values and goals, and take initiative to navigate through challenges rather than passively reacting to circumstances.

Commitment: The third "C" represents a strong sense of commitment, determination, and perseverance in pursuing one's goals and values, even in the face of challenges. Resilient individuals have a clear sense of purpose and direction, and they remain dedicated and committed to their goals, even when obstacles arise. They demonstrate resilience by staying focused, motivated, and taking consistent action towards what they value and believe in.

Purpose and Values: Commitment is grounded in a clear sense of purpose and alignment with personal values. Resilient individuals have a deep understanding of what matters to them and are committed to living in alignment with their values and goals, even when faced with challenges.

- Goal Orientation: Commitment involves setting and working towards meaningful goals. Resilient individuals set specific, achievable goals that are in line with their values and commit to taking consistent action to pursue and achieve those goals, despite setbacks or obstacles.
- Persistence and Perseverance: Commitment encompasses persistence and the willingness to keep going, even when faced with difficulties. Resilient individuals exhibit determination and resilience, staying focused on their goals and persevering through setbacks and obstacles.
- Motivation and Drive: Commitment includes intrinsic motivation and a strong drive to succeed. Resilient individuals have a deep internal motivation and passion for what they are pursuing, which fuels their commitment to keep going, even in challenging times.
- Resilient Mindset: Commitment is supported by a resilient mindset characterized by optimism, hope, and a belief in one's ability to overcome adversity. Resilient individuals maintain a positive outlook, view setbacks as temporary, and see challenges as opportunities for growth and learning.
- Adaptability in Pursuit of Goals: Commitment involves adaptability and flexibility in the pursuit of goals. Resilient individuals are willing to adjust their strategies, approaches, or even their goals themselves when necessary, while still staying committed to the underlying purpose.
- Consistency and Discipline: Commitment requires consistency and discipline in taking action towards one's goals. Resilient individuals develop habits and routines that support their progress and maintain a disciplined approach, even when faced with distractions or obstacles.

These three components work together to strengthen resilience. Viewing challenges as opportunities, maintaining a sense of control over one's responses, and staying committed to one's goals and values contribute to building and sustaining resilience in the face of adversity. By adopting a mindset that embraces challenges, focusing on what can be controlled, and staying dedicated to personal growth and aspirations,

Part I: Resilience for resilients

individuals can enhance their ability to bounce back and thrive in the face of difficulties.

Part I: Resilience for resilients

CHAPTER 3: Trans-generational resilience

The enduring resilience of survivors in the aftermath of the Genocide against the Tutsi is a testament to the human spirit's remarkable capacity to rebound from the darkest of times. Their journey following this horrific event is a narrative that warrants appreciation, honor, and celebration. It serves as a powerful illustration of how individuals can reclaim their lives even when hope seems elusive, and there appears to be no reason to continue. It is an extraordinary effort that deserves recognition and admiration.

In the midst of the Genocide against the Tutsi, my mother was merely 15 years old, and I have longed to share her story. There is a saying that one cannot truly comprehend what they have not experienced themselves. So, I invite you to listen to the voices of the children of survivors, for we are here to safeguard the memory of those we lost. My mother's family was comprised of five children, and they lived in close proximity to the children of her father's brother, who had married her mother's cousins. This arrangement led to the older children living with my mother's parents, while the younger ones stayed with her aunt. This division was made with great care, as the older parents were known for their exceptional child-rearing skills, despite the fact that the younger couple was also adept at caring for the children.

I often find myself repeating the names of my mother's siblings who perished in the Genocide against the Tutsi 1994, both from her own family and from the other family I mentioned. Occasionally, I try to coax her into talking about them, hoping to preserve their memory. They had affectionate nicknames, and I am grateful that I can recall each one. The pain of losing someone close to you is something that resonates with all, and even reading these words may evoke that heartache. Now, imagine losing two or more loved ones in the blink of an eye, leaving you utterly alone. The survivors' journey to rebuild their lives was exceptionally challenging, and my mother emerged from this ordeal with four of her siblings from both families. It is easy to forget that they also had numerous aunts, uncles, and grandparents on both sides. I aspire to document her story in a book, ensuring that the names of her parents, relatives, and grandparents are preserved for future generations. Those innocents were brutally taken from us simply for who they were.

My father's mother, or as I'd like to affectionately refer to her, my grandmother, was a remarkable woman. She possessed qualities of humility, cheerfulness, and was a loving mother. My mother recounted how he celebrated each of his children's birthdays without exception, and to this day, birthdays hold a special place in her heart. He was also a devoted husband, and one story remains etched in my memory. On April 7, 1994, when the Genocide against the Tutsi began, my mother's family lived in Kanombe, near the President's Residence. They were among the first to be targeted. However, as the militia arrived to execute them, their father was not present. He had left early that morning in search of a larger vehicle to transport the family away, sensing that the day would not bode well. Upon his return, he discovered the unimaginable – his entire family had been mercilessly killed. My mother, hidden in a toilet nearby, could hear his footsteps approaching. When he saw the horrific scene, he cried out for his wife, unaware that his children also lay lifeless. My mother tried to persuade him to flee, but he was overcome with grief. He took his time mourning his wife without realizing that he was the next target. This tragic episode underscores the profound sorrow and agony experienced by widows and widowers of the Genocide against the Tutsi. Yet, they remain shining examples of resilience.

My maternal grandmother was named Kayitesi Theresa. My mother often spoke of her in reverent tones, even mentioning how she would name her business 'St. Theresa' if given the chance. Theresa was a kind, intelligent, and noble woman. She was taken from us at a young age, and my mother would often observe women of her age and remark how young her own mother would still be. The pain and nostalgia in my mother's voice when she described life with her mother are palpable. I can't help but mention that my grandmother was also incredibly beautiful. Regrettably, the only photograph of her that existed was brought by my uncle when I was just five years old. They intended to use it for a commemoration, but inexplicably, it vanished, leaving only memories. If my recollection serves me correctly, I can still see her face in my mind's eye.

I share these recollections to emphasize how resilience can be transmitted from one generation to the next. After the Genocide against the Tutsi, my mother, at the tender age of 15, became the eldest among the five surviving children. One of her sisters was not with them, and they were uncertain of her fate. The challenges they faced were immense, and it's worth noting that my mother initially attended Lycee de Kigali, an esteemed school where even the president's children studied. However, circumstances forced her to search for alternative educational opportunities. Despite the obstacles, hardships, and the responsibility of raising her younger siblings, she persevered in her pursuit of education.

In a mere four years, she was married and became a mother to me. The hardships she endured during this period cannot be understated. The Genocide against the Tutsi robbed children of their innocence and childhood. Not having her parents present at her wedding was a painful reminder of the past. Yet, she embraced her role as the advisor on how to raise her siblings and her own child with grace and determination. My mother's resilience is a testament to her strength, and she played a pivotal role in shaping me into the person I am today. The stories of other survivors who navigated the challenging aftermath of the Genocide are equally heart-wrenching, but they all share the common thread of resilience.

During my childhood, my mother rarely spoke about her own experiences unless she was in the company of other elders. It wasn't until my twenties that I began to ask her extensively about her life. I am grateful that I can now learn more about her childhood and the trials she faced. Mom, if you're reading this, know that I am endlessly proud of your journey of resilience. You are my inspiration to learn about other survivors, write this book, and appreciate the remarkable strength that resides within you.

Part I: Resilience for resilients

As I pursued my studies at the University of Rwanda, I became involved with organizations dedicated to the mental health of children from diverse backgrounds, particularly those who had faced adversity in their early years. My passion for mental health led me to believe that our childhood experiences shape who we become, and caring for children's mental well-being is crucial, especially for those who have endured hardships.

One day, while heading to my dormitory, I encountered a young girl who was pregnant. Despite being older than her, I struggled to find the right words to say. I quickly realized that asking why she was pregnant while studying would be insensitive. Fortunately, she approached me and said, in a soft voice, "I was coming to see you." We went to my room together, where we joined several colleagues on the balcony. My curiosity got the best of me, and I asked her how she managed to continue her studies in such circumstances. That day, she shared her entire story, explaining why she was pregnant at a young age and why she was determined to stay in school to secure a scholarship. I learned that she excelled academically. Words cannot fully convey the depth of understanding I gained that day. I began to think about her child's future and well-being, and I realized that her story was not unique. There were other girls like her.

From that moment on, I felt a calling to work with teen mothers who often faced abandonment by their families. I wanted to support them in maintaining their mental well-being while they worked hard to secure a better future for their families. This journey eventually led to the founding of the organization "Rise and Live," a name that encapsulates the essence of resilience.

When I shared this endeavor with my mother, her response surprised me. I had been hesitant to tell her about my plans, fearing that she might think I was too young for such a responsibility. However, after hearing my intentions, she said, "Those girls are me 21 years ago. I was in Senior Five when I became pregnant, and I missed only a few days of school before giving birth. I walked four kilometers every day. It wasn't easy." I, in my childlike curiosity, asked why she didn't stop attending school, to which she simply shook her head and left.

We are all products of our mothers' resilience, and we are driven to strive for the best in every aspect of life, refusing to settle for the easy path. The stories of survivors, the determination of teen mothers, and the unwavering support of our families all serve as reminders that resilience can be passed down through generations, inspiring us to rise and live, no matter the challenges we face.

CHAPTER 4: Spreading resilience

There are quite a few ways of spreading resilience, as I will show you below. We also spread it in many ways unknowingly in our everyday lives. Therefore, in this chapter, we will explore all of them to demonstrate that if it has happened, then you can rebound or spread your resilience light.

These are some ways of spreading resilience

Spreading resilience is a profound and far-reaching endeavor that extends beyond the confines of specific strategies or actions. It is a collective and continuous process that involves individuals, communities, and societies working together to build and sustain the ability to bounce back from adversity. While we have outlined some explicit ways to spread resilience, it's important to recognize that resilience is often shared inadvertently through our daily interactions and experiences.

One of the most compelling aspects of resilience is its contagious nature. When one person demonstrates resilience in the face of hardship, it can inspire and uplift those around them, creating a domino effect of strength and determination. It's like a spark that ignites a fire within a community, leading to a shared commitment to overcome challenges and emerge stronger.

Education and awareness are potent tools for spreading resilience intentionally. By equipping individuals with the knowledge and skills to navigate adversity, we empower them to confront life's difficulties with confidence. But it's equally important to remember that resilience often thrives in the sharing of personal stories, the willingness to listen, and the power of human connection.

Role modeling remains a pivotal means of spreading resilience. When someone in a community displays resilience, it not only serves as an inspiration but also sets a standard for how challenges can be faced. Others are encouraged to follow suit, knowing that resilience is not an innate trait but a skill that can be developed and honed.

Part I: Resilience for resilients

Promoting a positive mindset amplifies the impact of resilience. When individuals embrace the idea that setbacks are opportunities for growth and learning, they are more likely to persevere in the face of adversity. This shift in mindset not only builds individual resilience but also contributes to a culture of resilience within a community.

In the narrative of resilience, we often find that the stories of survivors, like those who endured the Genocide against Tutsi, carry a unique power. Their stories remind us of the indomitable strength of the human spirit and serve as beacons of hope. Writing letters of appreciation to these survivors not only acknowledges their resilience but also spreads a message of compassion and solidarity, transcending borders and cultures.

In essence, spreading resilience is an ongoing journey that involves conscious efforts and organic moments of support and understanding. It's about nurturing a collective spirit of resilience that can weather even the most challenging storms. By recognizing, appreciating, and learning from the resilience of individuals and communities, we can contribute to a world where strength, hope, and determination flourish in the face of adversity.

CHAPTER 5: Choosing to rebound

Choosing to rebound or bounce back from adversity is a powerful decision that can contribute to building resilience. Here are some steps individuals can take to choose to rebound:

- Acknowledge the setback: Recognize and acknowledge the adversity or setback that you have experienced. Denying or avoiding the reality of the situation can hinder the rebounding process. It's important to face the situation head-on and accept that a setback has occurred.

  Give yourself permission: Understand that setbacks happen to everyone at some point, and it is normal to experience setbacks and challenges. Give yourself permission to acknowledge and accept the setback without judgment or self-blame.

  Face the reality: Avoidance or denial of the setback can prolong the healing process. Instead, confront the reality of the situation and recognize the impact it has had on your life or goals. Be honest with yourself about the setback and its consequences.

  Validate your emotions: Allow yourself to experience and process the emotions that arise from the setback. It's natural to feel a range of emotions such as disappointment, frustration, or sadness. Validate these emotions as normal and give yourself the space to work through them.

  Journaling or reflection: Engage in self-reflection or journaling to explore your thoughts and feelings about the setback. Write down your thoughts, concerns, and any insights gained from the experience. This can help you gain clarity and better understand the situation.

  Seek support: Reach out to trusted friends, family, or a support network to share your experience and seek emotional support. Discussing the setback with others who can provide empathy, guidance, or a fresh perspective can be helpful in acknowledging and processing it.

Identify the impact: Reflect on how the setback has affected your life, goals, or aspirations. Consider the changes or adjustments that may be necessary as a result. Identifying the impact of the setback can help you understand its significance and begin to plan for recovery.

Take ownership: Accept personal responsibility for your role in the setback. This doesn't mean blaming yourself excessively, but rather recognizing any factors that you can learn from or improve upon. Taking ownership empowers you to make changes and move forward.

Learn from the setback: Embrace the setback as an opportunity for growth and learning. Consider what lessons can be gleaned from the experience. Reflect on the factors that contributed to the setback and explore how you can apply these insights to prevent similar situations in the future.

Reframe the setback: Shift your perspective on the setback by reframing it in a more positive light. Look for potential silver linings, hidden opportunities, or unexpected benefits that may have emerged from the setback. Reframing can help you find meaning and purpose in the experience.

Create a plan: Develop a plan for moving forward. Outline specific actions or steps you can take to address the setback and work towards recovery. Breaking down the plan into manageable tasks can make the process feel more achievable and help you regain a sense of control.

- Allow yourself to process emotions: Give yourself permission to experience and process the emotions that come with the setback. It's normal to feel a range of emotions such as disappointment, frustration, or sadness. Acknowledge these emotions and allow yourself to work through them in a healthy way.

Seek professional help: Consider working with a mental health professional who specializes in trauma and post-Genocide healing. They can provide a safe and supportive space for you to process your emotions and guide you through the healing journey.

Connect with support networks: Reach out to support networks and communities of survivors who have had similar experiences. Sharing your story and listening to others can provide validation, understanding, and a sense of belonging.

Practice self-compassion: Be gentle and patient with yourself as you navigate the emotions and memories associated with the Genocide. Understand that healing takes time and that it's okay to experience a range of emotions.

Create a safe and supportive environment: Surround yourself with people who are understanding, empathetic, and supportive. Limit exposure to triggers that may intensify distressing emotions and memories.

Express your emotions: Find healthy ways to express your emotions, such as through journaling, art, music, or talking with a trusted confidant. Allow yourself to express your feelings openly and honestly without judgment.

Educate yourself: Learn about the psychological and emotional effects of trauma and Genocide. Understanding the common reactions and coping strategies can help you make sense of your own experiences and emotions.

Engage in self-care: Prioritize self-care activities that promote your physical, mental, and emotional well-being. This can include activities such as exercise, relaxation techniques, engaging in hobbies, spending time in nature, and connecting with loved ones.

Practice mindfulness: Incorporate mindfulness techniques into your daily routine to help ground yourself in the present moment. Mindfulness can help manage overwhelming emotions and promote a sense of calm and clarity.

Seek validation and validation: Find ways to validate your experiences and emotions. This can involve seeking validation from others who understand the historical context and impact of the Genocide or engaging in self-validation by recognizing and honoring your own strength and resilience.

Honor your journey: Understand that the process of processing emotions and healing from such a traumatic experience is unique to each individual. Respect your own pace and allow yourself to heal in your own way.

- Reframe the situation: Shift your perspective and reframe the setback as an opportunity for growth and learning. Look for any silver linings or lessons that can be gained from the experience. By reframing the situation, you can start to see it as a stepping stone towards personal development and new possibilities.

Acknowledge the historical context: Educate yourself about the historical and sociopolitical factors that led to the Genocide against the Tutsi. Understanding the larger context can help you see your experience as part of a larger narrative of resilience and survival.

Recognize your strength and resilience: Reflect on the strength and resilience that allowed you to survive the Genocide. Recognize that you have overcome immense challenges and demonstrate incredible courage in the face of extreme adversity.

Emphasize your identity and culture: Embrace and celebrate your Tutsi identity and culture. Recognize the richness and resilience of the Tutsi community, which has endured and thrived despite the horrors of the Genocide. Your identity and heritage are powerful sources of strength and resilience.

Find meaning and purpose: Explore ways to find meaning and purpose in your survival. Consider how your experience can inspire and empower others, raise awareness about the Genocide, or contribute to efforts for justice, reconciliation, or prevention of future atrocities.

Share your story: Sharing your story with trusted individuals or through platforms such as memoirs, art, or public speaking can help you reclaim your narrative and inspire others. By sharing your experiences, you raise awareness, foster empathy, and create opportunities for healing and understanding.

Seek support and connect with other survivors: Connect with other survivors of the Genocide against the Tutsi. Sharing your experiences and engaging in supportive communities can provide validation, understanding, and a sense of belonging. Collaborating with others who have similar experiences can also empower collective healing and resilience.

Engage in advocacy and activism: Consider becoming involved in advocacy or activism efforts related to Genocide prevention, human rights, or reconciliation. Working towards justice and raising awareness can provide a sense of purpose and contribute to reframing the narrative.

Focus on rebuilding and healing: Shift your focus towards rebuilding your life and engaging in healing practices. This may involve seeking professional support from therapists or counselors who specialize in trauma and post-Genocide healing.

Practice self-care: Prioritize self-care as you navigate the process of reframing. Engage in activities that bring you joy, nurture your well-being, and promote your overall physical and mental health. Take time to rest, reflect, and engage in practices that replenish your energy.

Embrace hope and resilience: Embrace a mindset of hope and resilience. Recognize that despite the atrocities you have endured, you have the capacity to rebuild, heal, and create a positive future. Cultivate optimism and a belief in your ability to overcome challenges and contribute to positive change.

- Set goals and create a plan: Establish clear goals that you want to achieve as you rebound from the setback. These goals can be small and manageable steps that move you forward. Create a plan of action that outlines the specific actions you need to take to reach your goals. Having a roadmap helps provide direction and focus during the rebounding process.

Reflect on your aspirations: Take time to reflect on your personal aspirations, interests, and values. Consider what you are passionate about, what brings you joy, and what you want to achieve in various aspects of your life.

Identify your strengths: Recognize your unique strengths, skills, and talents. Reflect on the qualities that have helped you overcome challenges and thrive despite the adversity you have experienced as a survivor or child of survivors.

Define your short-term and long-term goals: Set both short-term and long-term goals that align with your aspirations. Short-term goals can be achievable within a few months to a year, while long-term goals may take several years to accomplish. Ensure your goals are specific, measurable, attainable, relevant, and time-bound (SMART).

Break down your goals: Break down your long-term goals into smaller, manageable steps. These smaller steps will serve as milestones along the way and help you stay motivated and focused.

Prioritize your goals: Determine the priority of each goal based on its importance and urgency. Consider which goals will have the most significant impact on your personal growth, well-being, or the causes you are passionate about.

Create an action plan: Outline the specific actions you need to take to achieve each goal. Consider what resources, skills, or support you might need along the way. Be detailed and specific in your action plan to ensure clarity and direction.

Seek support and resources: Identify the support systems and resources available to help you in pursuing your goals. This can include mentors, community organizations, educational institutions, professional networks, or counseling services. Reach out to these resources for guidance, advice, or practical assistance.

Monitor your progress: Regularly monitor your progress towards your goals. Assess and adjust your action plan as needed. Celebrate the milestones you achieve along the way, and use any setbacks as learning opportunities to refine your approach.

Stay resilient and flexible: Recognize that setbacks and challenges are a normal part of any journey. Cultivate a resilient mindset that allows you to adapt, learn from setbacks, and persevere in the face of obstacles. Stay flexible in your approach, as circumstances may change and require adjustments to your plan.

Practice self-care: Prioritize self-care as you work towards your goals. Take care of your physical, mental, and emotional well-being. Engage in activities that recharge you, manage stress effectively, and maintain a healthy work-life balance.

- Cultivate a resilient mindset: Adopt a mindset of resilience by cultivating positive thoughts and beliefs. Embrace optimism, self-belief, and a growth mindset. Remind yourself that setbacks are temporary and that you have the strength and ability to overcome challenges. Focus on your strengths and previous successes to bolster your confidence.

Acknowledge your strength: Recognize and acknowledge the strength and resilience that allowed you to survive and navigate the challenges you faced as a Genocide survivor. Remind yourself of your inner resilience and the courage you have shown in overcoming adversity.

Embrace your story: Embrace your identity as a Genocide survivor and the unique experiences that have shaped you. Understand that your story is powerful and can inspire others. Recognize the wisdom and strength that comes from surviving such a traumatic event.

Practice self-compassion: Be kind and compassionate towards yourself. Treat yourself with the same empathy and understanding that you would offer to a loved one. Acknowledge that it is natural to have challenging emotions or moments of vulnerability, and allow yourself the space to heal and grow.

Reframe challenges as opportunities for growth: Shift your perspective on challenges and setbacks. View them as opportunities for personal growth and learning. Recognize that you have already demonstrated resilience by surviving the Genocide, and this resilience can continue to guide you through future challenges.

Foster a supportive network: Surround yourself with a supportive community of individuals who understand and validate your experiences as a Genocide survivor. Seek connections with others who have shared similar journeys, as they can provide understanding, encouragement, and a sense of belonging.

Seek professional support: Consider seeking professional help from therapists or counselors who specialize in trauma and post-Genocide healing. They can provide valuable guidance, tools, and techniques to help you cultivate resilience and navigate the specific challenges you may face as a Genocide survivor.

Practice gratitude: Cultivate a practice of gratitude by regularly acknowledging and appreciating the positive aspects of your life. Focus on the present moment and identify the things you are grateful for, no matter how small. Gratitude can help shift your mindset towards a more positive and resilient outlook.

Develop coping strategies: Explore and develop coping strategies that work for you. This may include techniques such as deep breathing, mindfulness, journaling, creative expression, or engaging in activities that bring you joy and promote well-being. Find healthy ways to process and manage difficult emotions that may arise.

Set realistic goals: Set realistic goals that align with your aspirations and values. Break them down into smaller, achievable steps. Each small success along the way will build your confidence and reinforce your resilience.

Embrace self-care: Prioritize self-care as a foundational element of your resilience. Take care of your physical, emotional, and mental well-being by engaging in activities that recharge and nourish you. This can include exercise, adequate rest, healthy nutrition, spending time in nature, pursuing hobbies, or seeking out moments of peace and solitude.

Remember, cultivating a resilient mindset is a journey that requires patience, self-compassion, and ongoing practice. Be patient with yourself as you navigate the complexities of your experiences and honor the strength and resilience that already resides within you.

- Seek support: Reach out to your support system for encouragement, guidance, and perspective. Share your experience with trusted friends, family, or mentors who can offer support and advice. Surrounding yourself with a positive and understanding network can provide the emotional support needed to rebound effectively.

Recognize the need for support: Acknowledge that you may benefit from support to help you process your experiences, emotions, and any challenges you may be facing. Understand that seeking support is a sign of strength and a proactive step towards healing.

Find a trusted individual: Identify a trusted individual in your life who can provide a listening ear, empathy, and support. This could be a family member, friend, mentor, or spiritual leader. Choose someone who is non-judgmental and understanding, and whom you feel comfortable opening up to.

Connect with survivor communities: Seek out survivor communities or organizations that provide support specifically for Genocide survivors. These communities can offer a safe space for sharing experiences, connecting with others who have had similar experiences, and accessing resources and services tailored to the needs of survivors.

Seek professional help: Consider working with a mental health professional who specializes in trauma and post-Genocide healing. They can provide specialized support and therapeutic interventions to help you navigate the unique challenges you may face as a Genocide survivor. Look for professionals experienced in working with trauma survivors or those familiar with the specific cultural context and historical background of the Genocide.

Attend support groups or therapy sessions: Join support groups or therapy sessions specifically designed for survivors of Genocide or trauma. These groups provide a supportive and understanding environment where you can share your experiences, learn coping strategies, and connect with others who have gone through similar experiences.

Access community resources: Research and connect with community resources that provide support to survivors of Genocide. These resources may include counseling services, legal support, advocacy organizations, or cultural and community centers that offer programs and activities for survivors.

Utilize helplines and hotlines: Take advantage of helplines and hotlines that provide support and crisis intervention services. These services can offer immediate support during times of distress or when you need someone to talk to.

Explore online support networks: Engage in online support networks and forums where survivors of Genocide connect and share their experiences. These platforms can provide a sense of community, support, and information from the comfort of your own home.

- Take action: Take proactive steps towards rebounding and achieving your goals. Start implementing the plan you created and take small, consistent actions that move you forward. Celebrate each milestone and use them as fuel to keep pushing forward.

Define your purpose: Clarify what motivates you and what specific issues or causes you feel passionate about as a Genocide survivor. This could include justice, human rights, reconciliation, education, or advocacy for Genocide prevention.

Educate yourself: Continuously educate yourself about the Genocide, its historical context, and its impact. Stay informed about relevant social, political, and cultural developments related to the Genocide. This knowledge will provide a strong foundation for taking informed action.

Connect with survivor networks: Reach out to survivor networks, organizations, or communities that are dedicated to supporting Genocide survivors. Connecting with others who have similar experiences can provide solidarity, validation, and a sense of belonging. It can also offer opportunities for collective action and collaboration.

Share your story: Consider sharing your personal story as a Genocide survivor. This can be done through various mediums such as writing, public speaking, art, or multimedia platforms. Sharing your story raises awareness, challenges misconceptions, and fosters empathy and understanding.

Advocate for justice: Advocate for justice by supporting efforts to hold perpetrators accountable for their actions. This may involve collaborating with human rights organizations, supporting legal initiatives, or advocating for the establishment of truth and reconciliation commissions.

Engage in community reconciliation: Participate in community reconciliation initiatives aimed at healing wounds and fostering unity. This can include attending memorial events, participating in dialogue sessions, and engaging in community-led projects focused on healing and rebuilding.

Support survivors and their families: Extend support to fellow survivors and their families. This can be done through offering emotional support, providing practical assistance, or advocating for their needs. Building a strong support network among survivors can be a powerful source of resilience and collective action.

Engage in educational initiatives: Contribute to educational initiatives that promote understanding and awareness of the Genocide. This can involve speaking at schools, universities, or community events, supporting educational programs, or collaborating with educators to develop curriculum materials related to the Genocide.

Collaborate with organizations and institutions: Partner with local or international organizations, educational institutions, or government bodies to amplify your impact. Collaborating with established entities can provide resources, networks, and platforms to reach a broader audience and effect systemic change.

Engage in advocacy and fundraising: Advocate for Genocide prevention, human rights, and support for survivors by engaging in advocacy campaigns and fundraising efforts. This can include lobbying for policy changes, raising funds for organizations supporting survivors, or organizing fundraising events.

- Practice self-care: Prioritize self-care as you rebound from a setback. Take care of your physical, mental, and emotional well-being. Engage in activities that bring you joy, practice stress management techniques, get adequate rest, and nourish your body with healthy habits. Taking care of yourself ensures you have the energy and resilience to rebound effectively.

Prioritize your physical health: Take care of your physical health by engaging in regular exercise, eating nutritious foods, and getting enough rest and sleep. Physical activity can help reduce stress, improve mood, and boost overall well-being.

Seek professional support: Consider working with a mental health professional who specializes in trauma and post-Genocide healing. They can provide guidance, therapeutic interventions, and support tailored to your specific needs as a Genocide survivor.

Create a support system: Surround yourself with a supportive network of friends, family, or fellow survivors who understand and validate your experiences. Share your thoughts, feelings, and concerns with trusted individuals who can provide empathy and support.

Practice mindfulness and relaxation techniques: Engage in mindfulness practices such as meditation, deep breathing exercises, or yoga. These techniques can help you stay present, manage stress, and cultivate inner peace and resilience.
Engage in activities that bring you joy: Dedicate time to activities that bring you joy and provide a sense of fulfillment. This could include hobbies, creative outlets, spending time in nature, listening to music, or engaging in cultural practices that resonate with you.

Set boundaries: Establish clear boundaries to protect your emotional well-being. Learn to say no when necessary and prioritize your needs and limitations. This includes setting boundaries with people, situations, and activities that may trigger difficult emotions or overwhelm you.

Engage in self-reflection and journaling: Set aside time for self-reflection and journaling. Reflect on your thoughts, feelings, and experiences as a means of processing and understanding your emotions. Writing can be a therapeutic outlet and a way to gain insight into your healing journey.

Practice self-compassion: Be gentle and compassionate with yourself. Recognize that healing takes time and that it's normal to have ups and downs along the way. Treat yourself with kindness, understanding, and acceptance, just as you would treat a loved one.

Engage in acts of self-nurturing: Engage in activities that nurture and replenish your mind, body, and soul. This can include taking relaxing baths, practicing self-massage, engaging in hobbies, spending time in nature, or enjoying moments of solitude and reflection.

Learn from the experience: Reflect on the setback and identify the lessons or insights it has provided. Use this knowledge to grow and develop as an individual. Consider what changes or adjustments you can make moving forward to prevent similar setbacks in the future.

Stay persistent and resilient: Rebounding from a setback takes time and effort. Stay persistent in your efforts and remain resilient in the face of challenges. Keep a long-term perspective and remind yourself of your goals and the progress you've made. Embrace the resilience within you and continue to bounce back, even in the face of future obstacles.
Remember that resilience is a journey, and it may have ups and downs. Be patient with yourself, celebrate your resilience, and recognize that it is normal to face setbacks along the way. With persistence, self-care, support, and a positive mindset, you can continue to cultivate resilience as a Genocide survivor.

CHAPTER 6: What doesn't kill you makes you stronger

"What doesn't kill you makes you stronger" is a popular phrase that encapsulates the concept of resilience and personal growth through adversity. It suggests that facing and overcoming challenges can lead to increased strength, resilience, and personal development.

The phrase implies that going through difficult experiences can actually be transformative and can build inner strength and resilience. It suggests that by navigating and surviving adversity, individuals can gain valuable life lessons, develop coping skills, and discover their own inner resources.

However, it's important to note that the phrase is not meant to trivialize or dismiss the pain and struggles that individuals face in difficult situations. Everyone's experiences and responses to adversity are unique, and it's essential to acknowledge and validate the impact of challenging circumstances.

Ultimately, the phrase serves as a reminder that even in the face of adversity, individuals have the capacity to overcome and grow from their experiences, ultimately becoming stronger and more resilient as a result.

As a Genocide survivor, the phrase "what doesn't kill you makes you stronger" can take on a complex and nuanced meaning. It acknowledges the immense trauma and suffering experienced during the Genocide against the Tutsi, while also highlighting the resilience and strength that survivors possess.

For Genocide survivors, the phrase can signify the ability to endure and persevere through unimaginable horrors. It recognizes the extraordinary resilience and determination demonstrated by individuals who have survived such a traumatic event.

However, it's important to approach this phrase with sensitivity and respect for the individual experiences of Genocide survivors. Each person's journey and healing process is unique, and it's crucial to recognize that not all survivors may resonate with the idea that their experiences have made them stronger.

Survivors of Genocide often carry deep emotional wounds and may grapple with ongoing trauma, grief, and other challenges long after the Genocide has ended. Their resilience should not be measured solely by their ability to endure, but also by their ability to heal, seek support, and rebuild their lives in the aftermath.

It is essential to approach the topic with empathy, understanding, and a recognition of the ongoing complexities and long-term effects of Genocide on survivors. The phrase can serve as a reminder of the resilience and strength that can emerge from adversity, but it should be understood in the broader context of the survivors' experiences and the ongoing healing process they undertake.

Ultimately, the phrase should be understood within the context of the individual survivor's experiences, perspectives, and personal journey of healing and resilience. It is a deeply personal and nuanced concept that may vary from person to person.

CHAPTER 7: Resilience as a background rhythm of every beat

Resilience can indeed be seen as a background rhythm that underlies every beat of life. It is the capacity to bounce back, adapt, and thrive in the face of adversity, setbacks, and challenges. Like a steady rhythm, resilience provides a foundation that supports and sustains individuals through difficult times.

Just as a rhythmic beat gives structure and stability to a song, resilience provides a sense of stability and strength in navigating life's ups and downs. It allows individuals to maintain their balance, remain grounded, and keep moving forward even in the face of difficult circumstances.

Resilience is not a one-time event but a continuous process that becomes ingrained in a person's mindset and actions. It is the underlying rhythm that guides individuals to persevere, find solutions, and learn from experiences. It helps individuals adapt to change, recover from setbacks, and embrace new opportunities.

Just as a beat in music can be uplifting and energizing, resilience can inspire and motivate individuals to keep going, even when faced with overwhelming challenges. It instills a sense of hope, determination, and belief in one's ability to overcome obstacles and thrive.

Moreover, like the background rhythm in music, resilience can provide a sense of coherence and connection in one's life. It helps individuals integrate their experiences, emotions, and lessons learned, creating a harmonious and meaningful narrative of personal growth and transformation.

While the intensity of the beat may vary throughout different stages of life, resilience remains an underlying presence, supporting individuals in their journey. It becomes a part of one's character, shaping their responses, choices, and overall approach to life.

Part I: Resilience for resilients

Resilience can be likened to a background rhythm that permeates every beat of life. It provides stability, motivation, and strength, allowing individuals to navigate challenges, adapt to change, and thrive in the face of adversity.

For survivors, resilience becomes a foundational aspect of their journey. It is the underlying rhythm that sustains them, even in the face of ongoing challenges and triggers related to their experiences. It is the internal strength that allows them to continue moving forward, healing, and rebuilding their lives.

Similar to the steady beat in music, resilience provides survivors with a sense of stability, grounding, and continuity. It serves as a guiding force that helps them maintain their balance, cope with triggers, and find ways to thrive despite the lingering effects of trauma.

Resilience in survivorship is not a one-time event but an ongoing process. It involves developing coping strategies, seeking support, and engaging in self-care to address the unique challenges and needs that arise. It is the rhythm of resilience that helps survivors adapt, recover, and find meaning and purpose in their lives beyond their traumatic experiences.

Furthermore, just as the background rhythm in music creates coherence and connection in a song, resilience in survivorship helps survivors make sense of their experiences, integrate their past into their present, and find a sense of continuity in their personal narratives. It allows them to connect with others who have shared similar experiences, fostering a sense of community and understanding.

While the intensity of the resilience rhythm may vary for each survivor and at different stages of the healing process, it remains a constant presence. It is the driving force that propels survivors forward, even during difficult times, and empowers them to reclaim their lives and create a new narrative of strength, growth, and survivorship.

Part I: Resilience for resilients

Instantly, in the context of survivorship, resilience as a background rhythm of every beat acknowledges the ongoing strength, adaptability, and perseverance of survivors as they navigate the aftermath of trauma. It provides stability, continuity, and a sense of coherence in their healing journey, enabling them to move forward, thrive, and reclaim their lives.

Every beat of our heart, every pulse of emotion, and every tremor of challenge is subtly directed by an unperceived metronome – resilience. In the symphony of life, where chaotic chords and uplifting melodies intertwine, resilience becomes the silent conductor that keeps every note in harmony.

Just as music flows in structured rhythms, life's journey oscillates between highs and lows. Amidst these variances, resilience acts as the metronome, ensuring the tune never falters. While the world listens to the overt melodies, the metronome of resilience works silently in the backdrop, setting the pace and maintaining order.

Imagine a dancer, gracefully moving through an intricate ballet routine. Behind the swirls, leaps, and poise, there is a hidden rhythm that guides each movement. This rhythm is resilience. As the dancer encounters obstacles, slips, or stumbles, it's the invisible rhythm of resilience that ensures they rise and continue their performance with even more fervor.

Drawing parallels with the story of survivors, their life resonates with these dance sequences. With every challenge, the rhythm of resilience guides them, not just helping them get back on their feet, but instilling a vigor to dance again with renewed spirit. As they pivot through their healing journey, resilience is the silent music sheet they refer to, ensuring their steps align with their path to recovery.

Often, we mistake resilience as just bouncing back. However, it's more than that. It's about synchronizing with the rhythm of life and ensuring one remains in harmony regardless of the discordant events. The essence of resilience is deeply embedded in every survivor's story, reminding them of their innate power to reset their rhythm even after being momentarily offbeat.

While life can sometimes seem off-beat and uncertain, the rhythm of resilience helps in finding one's groove again. Survivors, amidst their storms, find solace in this silent beat – it reminds them of their strength, their capability to innovate their dance moves, and their ability to turn even the harshest music into an anthem of victory.

So, as you journey through the pages of challenges, triumphs, and survival, remember the silent metronome of resilience, ever-present and ever-guiding. It's the backdrop to every story, every challenge, and every victory. Like the eternal rhythm governing the cosmos, resilience too, orchestrates our journey, ensuring that every beat resonates with hope, strength, and undying spirit.

CHAPTER 8: Resilience: The Heartbeat of Human Endurance

Consider the waves of the ocean, ceaselessly crashing upon the shores, only to retreat and gather strength to surge forward once again. This persistent ebb and flow can be seen as a reflection of human resilience. Each retreat represents moments of introspection, recovery, and gathering strength, while every forward surge symbolizes our innate drive to confront challenges head-on and to grow from them.

Resilience isn't a flat line, it's an undulating cadence that gives depth to our experiences, making each challenge a note in the grand composition of life. It's a rhythm so deeply embedded within us that sometimes we're not even aware of its presence. But it's there, driving our actions, molding our responses, and determining the texture of our experiences.

This rhythm is like a silent heartbeat, an intrinsic part of our existence. Even when life's music seems to drown in the cacophony of hardships, traumas, or losses, the rhythm of resilience provides the subtle undertone that nudges us to find our melody again.

As we delve deeper into the realm of survivors, we find that this rhythm is especially pronounced. Each individual carries their unique cadence of resilience. For some, it's a pulsating beat that pushes them to move swiftly past their traumas, while for others, it's a slow, methodical rhythm that gives them the space to heal, reflect, and grow at their own pace.

Survivors, much like masterful musicians, have an uncanny ability to tune into this rhythm even when everything around them seems discordant. They lean into their resilience, allowing it to guide their healing process, shape their narratives, and direct their future paths.

When a musician plays, it's not just about the notes that resonate but also about the pauses between them. Similarly, resilience isn't just about the triumphant moments of overcoming but also about the quiet moments of reflection, the pauses that give survivors the space to breathe, to understand, and to prepare for the next note in their life's symphony.

Part I: Resilience for resilients

It's important to understand that the rhythm of resilience doesn't demand a constant, forward-moving pace. Sometimes, it asks us to slow down, to pause, to reflect, and to gather ourselves. It's this balanced dance between motion and stillness, between facing challenges and retreating to heal, that paints the full picture of what resilience truly is.

In the grand tapestry of life, each thread of challenge, joy, setback, and triumph contributes to a design that is uniquely ours. And guiding the weaver's hand, ensuring that the pattern emerges as one of strength, beauty, and hope, is the ever-present rhythm of resilience, humming softly in the backdrop, orchestrating our every move.

Picture a forest that has endured a devastating wildfire. Even as the flames consume its trees and the thick smoke obscures the sky, beneath the charred surface, life persists. Seeds lie in wait, prepared to germinate and renew the forest once conditions are right. This revival, this undying spirit of nature, is much like the resilience inherent in each human soul.

Every aspect of nature – from the phoenix that rises from the ashes to the seasons that cyclically transform the earth – showcases resilience. These cycles and rhythms speak of renewal, revival, and an unwavering drive. In humans, this manifests as the innate ability to face adversities and evolve, each challenge faced adding a richer tone to the ongoing symphony of life.

The rhythm of resilience is not loud and brash but soft, persistent, and enduring. It's like the gentle tapping of rain on a windowpane or the continuous dripping of water that, over time, can wear away even the hardest of stones. It's quiet but relentless. Resilience doesn't shout; it whispers promises of tomorrow into the heart of the weary.

In the vast chronicles of survival, it's often these silent, small moments of resilience that become transformative. They remind survivors that they aren't defined by the hardships they face but by the courage they summon during those times. It's not the magnitude of the trauma but the subtle, steady rhythm of resilience that crafts the story.

Part I: Resilience for resilients

A mountain, unyielding and towering, faces countless storms, winds, and torrents. Yet, it stands tall, not because it's never challenged, but because its foundation is strong. Similarly, the resilient spirit of survivors rests on a foundation built from lessons learned, tears shed, and battles won. This foundation pulsates with a rhythm that continually drives them upwards, regardless of the weight of their past.

Every tear shed carves a deeper resonance into the rhythm of resilience, every sleepless night adds a layer of depth, and every moment of choosing hope over despair amplifies its melody. While the notes of pain, loss, and grief are undeniable, it's the rhythm of resilience that ensures the overall symphony is one of hope, recovery, and growth.

To truly grasp the essence of resilience, one must listen intently, not to the booming distractions of life but to the quiet, persistent drumbeat that underlies it all. It's in this attentive silence that one can hear the echoes of battles fought, challenges overcome, and the unyielding spirit of survival. In the dance of life, while circumstances may dictate the steps, it's the rhythm of resilience that composes the music.

CHAPTER 9: Resilience: The Silent Maestro of Human Spirit

In the vast theater of existence, where countless acts of joy, sorrow, growth, and stagnation play out, there's a silent maestro orchestrating the scenes - resilience. While the individual acts garner applause or tears, it's this maestro that ensures the show goes on, no matter how dramatic the plot twists become.

Imagine a river, winding its way through varying landscapes. At times, it meets mountains and is forced to chart a new course. Sometimes, it plummets down steep gorges, forming roaring waterfalls. There are moments when it expands, serene and vast, and others when it's just a meandering stream. Yet, through all these changes, it never stops. It constantly adapts, finding new paths, new depths, and new expressions. Such is the rhythm of resilience in our lives. It's an ever-adapting, ever-flowing force that ensures we continue to move forward, regardless of the terrains we encounter.

Each person's journey is filled with moments of sunshine and storms. There are highs, where one feels on top of the world, and lows, where the weight of the world seems unbearable. But, behind these moments, acting as the backdrop to every scene, is the consistent rhythm of resilience. It's the silent force that urges the heart to beat one more time, the mind to think one more thought, and the spirit to dream one more dream.

Life is not a straight path, and neither is resilience a constant drumbeat. It fluctuates, it adapts, it sometimes whispers and sometimes roars. But it never goes silent. Even in moments of profound grief or overwhelming joy, if one listens closely, the rhythm of resilience can be heard, maintaining the balance, offering a grounding force.

Survivors know this rhythm all too well. Their stories are not just tales of adversity but epics of endurance. When narrating their sagas, while they might recall the storms and thunders, the true essence lies in the spaces between - in the silent moments where they tapped into their reservoir of resilience. It's the soft hum that played as they stitched their wounds, the gentle lullaby that cradled them on sleepless nights, and the triumphant anthem that marked their milestones of recovery.

Resilience is not just the ability to bounce back; it's the strength to move forward, the wisdom to pivot, the grace to accept, and the courage to challenge. It's the unseen wind beneath the wings of those who soar after a fall. It's the silent song of the heart that's seen too much but still believes in more.

So, as life unfolds in its unpredictable cadence, and tales of triumph and trial interweave, remember to tune into that steadfast rhythm – the maestro of resilience. It's been there all along, choreographing the dance of existence, ensuring that every step, no matter how faltering, is a step forward in the grand ballet of life.

Survivorship: The Symphony of Resilient Souls

Survivorship is not merely a state of having endured; it's a testament to the spirit's relentless drive to persist, adapt, and flourish. This journey is underscored by a distinct rhythm, a symphony of resilience that orchestrates the dance of survival and thriving.

Imagine a phoenix. Mythical, yes, but emblematic of a survivor's spirit. Every descent into the ashes is not a culmination but a prelude. With each rise, the phoenix embodies a rejuvenation, an assertion of life and spirit, a testimony to the rhythm of resilience that never falters, even when faced with obliteration.

Survivors carry within them a mosaic of experiences. Each fragment, be it painful or uplifting, contributes to a larger tableau of endurance and resurgence. These pieces are held together by the resilient adhesive that survivors inherently possess. The rhythm of resilience is the heartbeat that infuses life into this mosaic, ensuring that the overall image is not one of brokenness, but of art, strength, and profound beauty.

Every survivor's narrative is unique, but the underlying cadence remains constant. It's a rhythm that often starts as a faint whisper, gradually growing in volume and tenacity. It speaks of hope in the darkest nights, strength in moments of vulnerability, and the transformative power of faith and perseverance.

In the world of survivorship, resilience is both the conductor and the composition. It dictates the pace at which survivors heal, adapt, and redefine their existence. There are moments of allegro, where hope and healing progress rapidly, and periods of adagio, where introspection and acceptance take center stage. Through each phase, the rhythm of resilience remains the guiding force, ensuring the symphony never loses its coherence.

For survivors, resilience is not a static trait but an evolving entity. It grows with every challenge faced, every tear shed, and every laugh shared. This rhythm is not merely background music; it's an anthem that defines their journey, a constant reminder of their ability to redefine narratives and emerge stronger.

When faced with adversities, survivors don't merely adapt; they transform. This transformation is underpinned by the persistent rhythm of resilience, encouraging them to not only endure but to re-envision, rebuild, and rejuvenate. It reminds them that survivorship isn't just about getting through the storm, but about learning to dance in the rain, finding the silver linings, and creating rainbows amidst the clouds.

Survivorship is a dance, an art form, an evolving journey where each step, twist, and turn is choreographed by the rhythm of resilience. It's an affirmation that no matter how cacophonous the past might have been, with resilience as the maestro, the future can still be a harmonious symphony of hope, growth, and triumphant resurgence.

In the vast tapestry of existence, survivorship stands out as a poignant testament to human spirit and perseverance. It's akin to a bud pushing through a crack in the pavement, defying all odds, driven by an innate desire to bloom. At the heart of this push, this drive, this resurgence, is the profound rhythm of resilience.

Part I: Resilience for resilients

The journey of a survivor often mirrors the cycles of nature. Just as winter, with its barrenness and desolation, gives way to the vibrancy and renewal of spring, survivors, too, transition from periods of profound darkness to moments of brilliant light. This cycle, with its dips and peaks, is harmonized by the ever-present rhythm of resilience, which underscores every challenge and triumph.

For survivors, resilience is more than just a mechanism to cope; it's the heartbeat that brings them back to life, time and time again. It's the silent mantra whispered in moments of doubt, the gentle lullaby that soothes pain, and the triumphant chorus that celebrates every victory, however small.

Within the realm of survivorship, this rhythm has many faces. It's the unwavering determination that fuels the pursuit of healing, the quiet strength that holds the fragments of a shattered past, and the hope that paints dreams of a brighter future. It's the force that propels survivors to rewrite their stories, not as tales of tragedy, but as epics of endurance and empowerment.

Survivorship, at its core, is about transformation. Like a caterpillar entering its chrysalis, survivors undergo moments of profound introspection, wrestling with pain, memories, and emotions. And then, driven by the unwavering rhythm of resilience, they emerge, not as who they were, but as evolved versions of themselves. Their scars, both visible and invisible, become marks of honor, testifying to battles fought and won.

Resilience, in the context of survivorship, is not a linear journey. It spirals, turns, retraces, and leaps forward. There are moments where the rhythm is a gentle hum, barely perceptible, guiding survivors through their darkest hours. At other times, it roars, a cacophony of strength and determination, propelling them towards newfound horizons of hope.

As the narrative unfolds, it becomes clear that resilience is not merely about enduring; it's about flourishing. It's about harnessing the lessons from the past to nurture the promise of tomorrow. Every tear becomes a stepping stone, every memory a guidepost, and every moment of despair a catalyst for growth.

In essence, survivorship is not just about moving past traumas; it's about embracing the rhythm of resilience, allowing it to shape, guide, and uplift. It's a dance between memory and hope, pain and purpose. In this delicate dance, resilience remains the ever-persistent beat, ensuring that each step, no matter how faltering, is a step towards rebirth, rejuvenation, and radiant resurgence.

CHAPTER 10: The Cultural Cornerstones of Resilience

Ubumuntu: The Essence of Humanity

Ubumuntu is a Bantu term that roughly translates to "I am because we are. Humanity." It embodies the idea that individual well-being and identity are inseparable from the well-being and identity of the community. In Rwandan culture, Ubumuntu is a fundamental belief that shapes social interactions, responsibilities, and values.

In the aftermath of the Genocide, Ubumuntu played a pivotal role in healing and reconciliation. Rwandans recognized that the wounds inflicted upon their society could only be addressed collectively. Through community dialogues, survivors and perpetrators engaged in difficult conversations, fostering understanding and empathy. This cultural value helped rebuild trust among neighbors, friends, and family members, paving the way for the nation's recovery.

The essence of humanity, encapsulated in concepts like "Ubumuntu " or "Ubumuntu," goes to the very heart of what it means to be human. It's a recognition that we are all interconnected, that our actions and well-being are intricately linked with those of others, our communities, and the broader world. This interconnectedness forms the bedrock of empathy and compassion, as we understand that the pain or joy of one individual has a ripple effect on the collective human experience.

Central to this essence is our capacity for empathy and compassion, the ability to genuinely understand and share in the emotions and experiences of others. These qualities drive us to support, uplift, and care for one another during moments of vulnerability and triumph, creating a sense of unity and shared responsibility.

The essence of humanity also extols the power of community and collaboration. It acknowledges that our most significant accomplishments often arise from collective efforts, where people come together to pursue common objectives. Communities serve as the cradle of culture, where traditions, values, and knowledge are passed down through generations, nurturing our shared human identity.

This essence encompasses altruism and sacrifice, the willingness to prioritize the needs of others above our own. Whether it's a parent's unwavering care for their child, a friend's selfless support, or the kindness of a stranger, these acts of selflessness highlight the deep well of compassion that resides within humanity.

Furthermore, it celebrates diversity in all its forms, recognizing that our differences are a source of strength rather than division. Embracing diversity and practicing inclusivity is essential for creating an environment where every individual feels valued, fostering a sense of belonging and shared humanity.

The essence of humanity also brings with it a profound sense of responsibility and stewardship for the planet and its inhabitants. It compels us to protect the environment, preserve biodiversity, and work towards a sustainable future for generations to come.

In the face of adversity, the essence of humanity shines through in our resilience and adaptability. It acknowledges our innate ability to overcome challenges, learn from difficulties, and evolve as individuals and communities.

Furthermore, it emphasizes the pursuit of knowledge, growth, and self-improvement, recognizing that as human beings, we are on a continuous journey of learning and development. This journey extends not only to personal growth but also to the betterment of society as a whole.

At its core, the essence of humanity is steeped in love, in all its forms. Love for family, friends, fellow humans, and oneself empowers us to form deep connections, derive meaning from our lives, and navigate the complexities of existence with grace and purpose. It reminds us that, at our very essence, we possess the capacity for kindness, understanding, and the betterment of both ourselves and the world around us.

Part I: Resilience for resilients

A hopeful future deeply rooted in the essence of Ubumuntu holds the promise of a more compassionate, empathetic, and harmonious world. As we embrace Ubumuntu, we envision a future where the interconnectedness of all humanity becomes a guiding principle for how we interact with each other and the planet.

In this hopeful future, communities across the globe recognize the intrinsic value of fostering strong bonds of solidarity and mutual support. People from diverse backgrounds come together, acknowledging that their individual well-being is inextricably linked to the well-being of others. This sense of collective responsibility transcends borders and fosters a global community that works collaboratively to address pressing issues, from climate change to social inequality.

In an Ubumuntu-inspired future, empathy and compassion are not just ideals but fundamental aspects of our daily lives. We prioritize understanding and caring for the experiences of others, ensuring that no one is left behind. This emphasis on empathy drives initiatives that alleviate suffering, promote social justice, and bridge divides between different communities and nations.

A hopeful future guided by Ubumuntu is one in which diversity is celebrated, not feared. We recognize that our differences enrich the human tapestry, and we honor and respect the unique contributions of each culture and individual. This celebration of diversity fosters a world where discrimination and prejudice are replaced by inclusivity and acceptance.

In this future, love and kindness are powerful forces for positive change. Acts of selflessness, altruism, and support are not just occasional occurrences but the norm. Love for family, friends, and humanity at large becomes the driving force behind efforts to build a more equitable and compassionate world.

Moreover, the essence of Ubumuntu inspires us to be stewards of the planet, ensuring a sustainable and flourishing future for generations to come. We recognize our role in preserving the environment and protecting the natural world, understanding that our well-being is intricately connected to the health of the Earth.

Ultimately, a hopeful future guided by Ubumuntu envisions a world where resilience, growth, and learning are embraced as essential components of our human journey. We understand that, even in the face of challenges, we possess the inner strength and collective wisdom to overcome adversity and create a brighter tomorrow.

In this future, the legacy of Ubumuntu is not confined to any one culture or region but becomes a universal philosophy that guides our interactions, policies, and institutions. It leads us toward a future where humanity thrives through unity, compassion, and a deep appreciation for the interconnectedness of all life.

In a hopeful future deeply rooted in Ubumuntu, we see the transformation of education and societal systems. Ubumuntu-inspired values are woven into the fabric of our schools and institutions, emphasizing not only academic excellence but also the development of empathy, compassion, and a sense of shared responsibility. Education becomes a means to nurture individuals who not only excel intellectually but also contribute positively to their communities and the world.

In this future, conflicts and disputes are resolved through dialogue and reconciliation, rather than violence or division. Communities and nations adopt restorative justice practices, following the example of Gacaca in Rwanda, to heal wounds, hold individuals accountable for their actions, and build bridges between conflicting parties. Ubumuntu's emphasis on forgiveness and understanding serves as a blueprint for resolving conflicts on both interpersonal and global scales.

Furthermore, a hopeful future guided by Ubumuntu recognizes the importance of economic and social justice. Policies and systems are designed to address disparities and ensure equitable access to resources, opportunities, and healthcare. The gap between the privileged and marginalized narrows, fostering a more inclusive society where the dignity and worth of every individual are upheld.

In this future, individuals are encouraged to lead lives of purpose and meaning, finding fulfillment not solely in material wealth but in the relationships they nurture, the contributions they make to their communities, and the positive impact they have on the world. The pursuit of happiness is redefined as the pursuit of a life lived in harmony with Ubumuntu's principles of interconnectedness, empathy, and compassion.

Moreover, technology and innovation are harnessed to amplify the positive aspects of Ubumuntu. Digital platforms and global connectivity enable people from all corners of the world to come together, share experiences, and collaborate on solutions to global challenges. Social media and communication tools are used to foster empathy, bridge cultural gaps, and promote cross-cultural understanding.

Ultimately, a hopeful future rooted in Ubumuntu envisions a world where the essence of humanity is celebrated and cherished as our most valuable asset. It is a world where individuals and societies recognize that our collective strength lies in our ability to uplift each other, protect the planet, and build a more just and compassionate global community. In this future, Ubumuntu is not just a philosophy but a lived experience that shapes the way we relate to one another and the world around us.

Kwibuka: Remembering and Honoring

Kwibuka, the Rwandan word for "remember," embodies the cultural commitment to never forget the horrors of the past. Through annual Kwibuka ceremonies, Rwandans honor the memory of the victims while reinforcing their determination to prevent such a tragedy from happening again. This act of remembrance is not just about grieving but also about drawing strength from the past to build a better future.

Part I: Resilience for resilients

In the context of a hopeful future deeply intertwined with the concept of Kwibuka, we envision a world that places a profound emphasis on remembrance, reconciliation, and the prevention of future atrocities.

In this future, Kwibuka serves as a powerful reminder of the lessons learned from history's darkest chapters. It is a global call to action, encouraging societies to acknowledge their past mistakes and work tirelessly to ensure that such atrocities are never repeated. Kwibuka ceremonies, not limited to Rwanda but held in nations worldwide, become annual events that unite people in commemorating not only the Genocide against the Tutsi but all instances of mass violence and discrimination.

Kwibuka-inspired education programs are integrated into school curricula worldwide. Students learn about the consequences of hatred and intolerance, as well as the importance of promoting peace, unity, and social justice. By teaching the history and lessons of Kwibuka, future generations are empowered to recognize early warning signs of conflict and discrimination, and to become advocates for change.

In this hopeful future, Kwibuka also inspires the creation of innovative initiatives and organizations dedicated to conflict prevention and peacebuilding. These entities draw from the resilience and determination of Rwandans to promote dialogue, reconciliation, and the strengthening of civil societies in regions affected by conflict. Kwibuka serves as a symbol of hope, showing that even in the aftermath of immense tragedy, healing and transformation are possible.

Moreover, Kwibuka ceremonies evolve to include not only mourning but also celebrations of unity and progress. They highlight the stories of survivors who have rebuilt their lives and the resilience of communities that have come together to heal. These gatherings serve as opportunities for healing and empowerment, as survivors share their experiences and inspire others to overcome adversity with strength and grace.

In this future, the global community acknowledges that remembrance is not a passive act but a proactive commitment to prevent the recurrence of Genocide and mass atrocities. Kwibuka serves as a beacon of hope, demonstrating that through collective remembrance, vigilance, and a dedication to peace, we can create a world where the horrors of the past remain in the past, and a brighter, more harmonious future awaits us all.

In a future deeply influenced by the essence of Kwibuka, the global community recognizes the significance of remembrance as a cornerstone of human progress. Kwibuka ceremonies, inspired by Rwanda's commitment to remember and honor the victims of the Genocide against the Tutsi, have evolved into a worldwide movement for acknowledging and learning from history's darkest moments.

These ceremonies serve as an annual reminder of the devastating consequences of hatred and division. They are not limited to Rwanda but have become a universal practice, held in nations and communities around the world. Kwibuka is no longer just about the Genocide against the Tutsi; it has expanded to commemorate all victims of mass violence, discrimination, and injustice, ensuring that their stories are never forgotten.

In this hopeful future, Kwibuka is deeply integrated into education systems. Schools globally incorporate lessons about the Genocide against the Tutsi and other historical atrocities into their curricula. Through these lessons, young minds are exposed to the devastating impact of prejudice and intolerance, as well as the importance of upholding human rights and promoting peace.

Kwibuka-inspired education empowers the next generation to recognize early warning signs of conflict, discrimination, and hatred. It equips them with the knowledge and tools to advocate for change, promote social cohesion, and prevent the escalation of violence in their communities and beyond.

Beyond education, Kwibuka inspires the creation of organizations and initiatives committed to conflict prevention, reconciliation, and peacebuilding. These entities draw from the resilience and determination of Rwandans to foster dialogue, heal deep-seated wounds, and strengthen civil societies in regions affected by conflict. The global network of Kwibuka-driven initiatives becomes a powerful force for positive change.

Kwibuka ceremonies, in this future, are not solely moments of mourning but also celebrations of unity and progress. They highlight the stories of survivors who have rebuilt their lives and the resilience of communities that have come together to heal. Kwibuka gatherings serve as platforms for healing, empowerment, and storytelling, where survivors share their experiences, inspiring others to overcome adversity with strength and grace.

Most importantly, Kwibuka embodies the global commitment to preventing the recurrence of Genocide and mass atrocities. It becomes a beacon of hope, demonstrating that through collective remembrance, vigilance, and a dedication to peace, we can create a world where the horrors of the past remain in the past. In this future, humanity stands united in its resolve to build a brighter, more harmonious world where the lessons of Kwibuka guide us toward lasting peace and understanding.

Resilience in Art and Music

Rwandan culture finds expression in vibrant art and music that capture the nation's spirit. Traditional dances like "Intore" showcase the resilience of the Rwandan people, with their graceful movements symbolizing the ability to rise above adversity. In songs and poetry, survivors share their stories, preserving their history and inspiring others to find hope and strength in their own narratives.

Resilience in art and music is a profound manifestation of the human spirit's resilience in the face of adversity. In a future where art and music take on an even more significant role in cultivating and expressing resilience, we witness a transformation in how these creative mediums are perceived and utilized.

Part I: Resilience for resilients

Art and music therapy programs expand and become globally recognized for their therapeutic value. These initiatives offer individuals dealing with trauma, stress, or emotional challenges a creative outlet for processing their experiences. The transformative power of art and music becomes a beacon of hope, helping people rebuild their lives by channeling their emotions into creative expression. These programs serve as sanctuaries of healing, where individuals can find solace, resilience, and a renewed sense of purpose.

Visual art, in particular, emerges as a compelling tool for storytelling. Artists from diverse backgrounds use their talents to depict narratives of resilience, survival, and the indomitable human spirit. Art exhibitions and galleries worldwide feature works that inspire empathy and contemplation. Viewers are encouraged to connect with the experiences of others, fostering a sense of solidarity and strength in shared stories of perseverance.

In the realm of music, resilience-themed compositions take center stage. Musicians and composers create songs that convey messages of resilience, unity, and empowerment. Concerts and festivals dedicated to such music attract global audiences, becoming platforms for collective healing and inspiration. The universal language of music transcends cultural boundaries, connecting people from all walks of life in their shared journey of resilience.

Art and music also play a crucial role in preserving cultural heritage and identity. Communities facing cultural threats, displacement, or loss due to conflict or environmental changes turn to artistic expression as a means of safeguarding their traditions. Through art and music, they ensure that their cultural resilience endures through generations, even in the face of adversity.

Beyond artistic expression, artists and musicians become advocates for social justice and change. They leverage their platforms to create art installations, music videos, and performances that raise awareness about pressing global issues, such as climate change, human rights violations, and social inequality. Their creative activism mobilizes support for critical causes, fostering resilience in the face of systemic challenges.

Moreover, art and music become bridges between cultures, facilitating collaborations that celebrate diversity and foster understanding. Artists and musicians from different backgrounds come together on projects that blend artistic traditions, creating powerful expressions of resilience that transcend borders and inspire global audiences. These collaborative efforts strengthen cultural bonds and promote cross-cultural empathy.

In education, art and music take on an expanded role in fostering resilience. Schools and community centers prioritize arts education as a means of nurturing creativity, self-expression, and emotional well-being. Students learn to channel their experiences into artistic forms, equipping them with valuable coping mechanisms for life's challenges. This emphasis on creative education empowers future generations to face adversity with resilience and a deep appreciation for the transformative power of art and music.

In this future, art and music cease to be mere forms of entertainment or expression; they become vital tools for human resilience. They provide individuals and communities with the means to heal, connect, and find strength in the beauty of creativity. Through these artistic expressions, people are reminded of their shared humanity and their capacity to triumph over adversity, making the world a more resilient and empathetic place.

Rebuilding Family and Community

In Rwandan culture, the family unit is of paramount importance, and communal bonds run deep. After the Genocide, countless Rwandans took on the role of caregivers, adopting orphaned children and supporting survivors who had lost their entire families. This sense of collective responsibility was not only a cultural imperative but also a pragmatic necessity for rebuilding society.

Part I: Resilience for resilients

Families and communities became the bedrock of resilience, offering emotional support, stability, and a sense of belonging. These bonds of love and solidarity were crucial in helping individuals heal from trauma and move forward with their lives.

Rebuilding family and community takes center stage in a future characterized by strong, resilient societies. At the heart of this vision is a concerted effort to fortify family bonds. Programs and resources aimed at strengthening familial relationships become widespread, ensuring that parents have the tools and support they need to foster healthy and loving connections with their children. Governments and organizations collaborate to provide financial assistance to families facing economic challenges, acknowledging that financial stability is a key factor in maintaining strong family ties. By prioritizing the well-being of families, societies in this future lay a sturdy foundation for resilience.

Community-centered initiatives play a pivotal role in fostering resilience. Neighborhood associations, local government programs, and grassroots organizations join forces to create safe, inclusive spaces where community members can connect, share resources, and offer support to one another. These initiatives aim to break down social isolation, fostering a profound sense of belonging and empowering individuals to actively contribute to the welfare of their communities. Communities become more than just geographical locations; they evolve into networks of mutual care and support.

Reimagining social services becomes a necessity in this future. Traditional social services are revamped to prioritize family and community well-being. Rather than solely focusing on crisis intervention, these services emphasize prevention and early intervention. Accessible mental health support, counseling, and family therapy help address issues before they escalate, equipping families and communities with the tools to navigate challenges effectively. By providing proactive assistance, societies create a buffer against crises.

Part I: Resilience for resilients

In this future, respect for elders and the transmission of intergenerational wisdom take on renewed significance. Older generations actively engage in mentoring and guiding younger community members. This intergenerational exchange of knowledge not only strengthens family bonds but also ensures that valuable lessons from the past are preserved and utilized for future resilience. Communities treasure the wisdom that comes with age, recognizing its pivotal role in nurturing resilience.

Community resilience centers become integral to the fabric of society. These centers offer a diverse range of services, from vocational training to mental health support, serving as hubs for community engagement. They provide spaces for educational workshops, cultural events, and social gatherings, becoming vital elements of community life. In these centers, the spirit of unity and collective responsibility thrives, further strengthening the social bonds that underpin resilience.

Restorative justice practices take precedence in this future. In cases of conflicts or disputes within families and communities, restorative justice principles guide the resolution process. Rather than resorting to punitive measures, these practices focus on repairing harm and rebuilding relationships. Dialogue, mediation, and reconciliation processes enable individuals to understand the impact of their actions and work towards healing. These practices promote forgiveness and understanding, nurturing resilience within communities.

Cultural diversity is celebrated and cherished as a source of strength. Communities host cultural festivals, food events, and heritage preservation initiatives that bring people together. These celebrations foster a profound sense of pride and belonging among community members, while also promoting cross-cultural understanding and cooperation. Embracing diversity enriches the social fabric, highlighting the importance of inclusivity and cultural appreciation in fostering resilience.

Part I: Resilience for resilients

Environmental stewardship becomes a shared commitment within communities. Initiatives like community gardens and renewable energy projects promote sustainability and ecological responsibility. By engaging in environmentally conscious practices, communities not only contribute to the planet's well-being but also strengthen their sense of collective responsibility. This environmental awareness underscores the interconnectedness of communities with the natural world, further fortifying their resilience.

Lastly, communities actively prepare for potential crises, whether they be natural disasters or economic challenges. Community-based emergency response teams are established, comprehensive evacuation plans are put in place, and support systems are arranged to assist vulnerable community members during times of crisis. This preparedness instills a sense of unity and shared responsibility among community members, empowering them to face adversity with resilience and determination.

In this future, the rebuilding of family and community emerges as a holistic approach to resilience, recognizing the profound interconnectedness of individuals within the larger social fabric. By nurturing family bonds, fostering community connections, and promoting a sense of collective responsibility, societies become better equipped to weather challenges and emerge stronger, more resilient, and more tightly knit than ever before.

In this future where the rebuilding of family and community takes precedence, the concept of resilience extends far beyond individual strength; it becomes a collective endeavor that permeates every facet of society.

Strengthened family bonds act as the cornerstone of resilience. Communities invest in family support systems, recognizing that the well-being of individuals within a family unit contributes significantly to the overall health of the community. Parenting programs and resources flourish, equipping caregivers with essential skills to nurture strong, loving relationships with their children. Financial assistance programs are designed to safeguard families from economic challenges, ensuring that financial stress doesn't jeopardize the bonds between family members. The commitment to strengthening families creates a web of emotional support that extends from the home to the broader community.

Community-centered initiatives thrive, transforming neighborhoods into hubs of resilience-building activities. Neighborhood associations, local government programs, and grassroots organizations collaborate to create safe, inclusive spaces where residents can connect and support one another. These initiatives encompass a spectrum of activities, from communal gardening projects to neighborhood watch programs. They foster a sense of belonging and shared responsibility, breaking down social isolation and empowering individuals to contribute actively to the welfare of their communities.

In this future, social services are reconfigured to place family and community well-being at the forefront. Services extend beyond crisis intervention, prioritizing prevention and early intervention. Accessible mental health support, counseling, and family therapy are readily available to address issues before they escalate. Families and communities gain the tools and resources to navigate challenges effectively, reducing the impact of crises and fostering resilience at both the micro and macro levels.

Intergenerational bonds are celebrated and valued, with older generations playing a pivotal role in mentoring and guiding younger community members. The wisdom passed down from elders enriches the lives of younger generations and reinforces the values that underpin resilient communities. The knowledge and experience of the elderly become cherished treasures, not only strengthening familial ties but also serving as a wellspring of resilience for the entire community.

Community resilience centers, equipped with a wide range of services, become bustling hubs of activity. These centers offer vocational training, mental health support, educational workshops, and cultural events. They become integral to community life, fostering a strong sense of unity and shared responsibility. Within these spaces, residents find not only the tools to address personal challenges but also opportunities to engage with their neighbors and build a tightly knit community that thrives on mutual support.

Restorative justice practices continue to gain traction in this future, emphasizing healing and reconciliation over punitive measures. Within families and communities, conflicts and disputes are resolved through dialogue, mediation, and reconciliation processes. This approach encourages individuals to take responsibility for their actions and fosters forgiveness and understanding. The result is not only the repair of fractured relationships but also a deeper sense of trust and resilience within the community.

The celebration of cultural diversity becomes a fundamental tenet of resilient communities. Cultural festivals, food events, and heritage preservation initiatives serve as platforms for residents to share their traditions and learn about the richness of others'. These celebrations instill pride and a sense of belonging, fostering cross-cultural understanding and cooperation. Embracing diversity strengthens the social fabric, reminding community members that their shared humanity transcends cultural differences.

Environmental stewardship is embraced as an integral aspect of community resilience. Initiatives like community gardens, renewable energy projects, and conservation efforts become community-wide endeavors. These practices not only promote sustainability and ecological responsibility but also reinforce the idea of shared responsibility for the planet. Communities recognize their interconnectedness with the natural world, reinforcing their resilience by ensuring the health of their environment.

Lastly, communities proactively prepare for potential crises, creating robust emergency response teams, evacuation plans, and support networks. Vulnerable community members are identified and safeguarded during times of crisis. Preparedness becomes a shared responsibility, instilling a sense of unity and collective resolve in the face of adversity.

In this future, the rebuilding of family and community represents a holistic approach to resilience, one that acknowledges the profound interconnectedness of individuals within the broader social tapestry. By nurturing family bonds, fostering community connections, and promoting a sense of collective responsibility, societies become not only more resilient but also more compassionate, tightly knit, and better equipped to face the challenges of an ever-changing world.

Icyizere - Hope: Despite the immense challenges faced by Rwanda, hope remains a cultural cornerstone. Rwandans draw strength from the belief that, with unity and determination, they can build a brighter future. Icyizere, or hope, serves as a guiding force that inspires resilience by encouraging individuals and communities to envision a better tomorrow and work tirelessly towards it.

In Rwandan culture, these cultural cornerstones serve as powerful foundations for resilience. They reflect a profound commitment to healing, reconciliation, and unity, demonstrating how cultural values and traditions can play a transformative role in rebuilding a society devastated by conflict and tragedy. These cornerstones continue to guide Rwanda's path toward a more resilient and harmonious future.

Icyizere, the cornerstone of hope in Rwandan culture, shines as a guiding light even in the darkest of times. It represents far more than just a concept; it is a powerful force that has played a transformative role in Rwanda's journey of healing and renewal.

In the aftermath of the Genocide against the Tutsi, when despair and trauma seemed insurmountable, icyizere emerged as a beacon of resilience. Rwandans, confronted with the immense weight of loss and suffering, found solace in the belief that hope could guide them towards a better future. It was a collective resolve that their nation could rise from the ashes and that unity and determination would pave the way.

Part I: Resilience for resilients

Icyizere empowers individuals and communities to envision a brighter tomorrow, even in the face of unimaginable adversity. It is the driving force that motivates survivors to rebuild their lives and propels communities to come together for reconciliation and progress. This hope is not passive but an active commitment to healing, unity, and the prevention of future atrocities.

Over the years, icyizere has been woven into the fabric of Rwandan society, shaping its institutions and policies. The nation's leadership, inspired by this cultural cornerstone, has pursued initiatives that prioritize social cohesion, education, and economic development. It recognizes that fostering hope is not just an abstract ideal but a pragmatic strategy for resilience and progress.

Icyizere is celebrated during Kwibuka, the annual commemoration of the Genocide. Where we pass on the candle light as the sign of Hope(Icyizere) While Kwibuka serves as a somber reminder of the past, it is also a testament to the enduring spirit of hope. Rwandans come together during this time to honor the memory of the victims and renew their commitment to preventing such atrocities from happening again. It is a poignant illustration of how hope, even in the face of profound tragedy, can be a catalyst for resilience and change.

Kwibuka, the annual commemoration of the Genocide, serves as a poignant reminder of the enduring power of icyizere. While it is a time of reflection on the horrors of the past, it is also a celebration of hope's triumph over despair. Rwandans gather during Kwibuka to honor the memory of the victims and renew their commitment to preventing such atrocities from happening again. It is a testament to the resilience that icyizere has nurtured, a living example of how hope can shape a nation's destiny.

The essence of icyizere extends beyond Rwanda's borders, serving as an inspiration to the global community. It demonstrates that even in the wake of the darkest chapters in human history, hope can prevail, and healing is possible. Rwanda's story of resilience, guided by icyizere, is a testament to the power of hope to transform societies and reaffirm the belief that a better future is attainable through unity, compassion, and unwavering determination.

Icyizere is not a passive or fleeting notion; it is an active, enduring commitment to healing, unity, and the prevention of future atrocities. It inspires individuals to rise above their own pain and trauma, to extend a hand of forgiveness, and to embrace a future built on reconciliation and hope. It empowers communities to come together, recognizing that their shared aspirations are far more potent than the forces that once sought to tear them apart.Icyizere, the radiant hope embedded in Rwandan culture, continues to illuminate the nation's path towards resilience, progress, and unity. As it flows through the collective consciousness of Rwandans, icyizere shapes not only individual aspirations but also the destiny of the nation itself.

In the wake of the Genocide against the Tutsi, icyizere emerged as a lifeline for a shattered society. It was the belief that, amid the darkness, there could still be light—a belief that would ultimately fuel Rwanda's remarkable transformation. In the midst of overwhelming despair, Rwandans clung to the conviction that they could rebuild their nation, heal deep wounds, and unite as one people. Icyizere became the driving force behind the determination to emerge from the abyss stronger and more resilient than ever before.

Rwanda's leadership, deeply influenced by icyizere, has forged a path of resilience and progress. Policies and initiatives prioritize social cohesion, education, and economic development, recognizing that a hopeful nation is a resilient nation. Icyizere is woven into the fabric of Rwandan institutions, guiding the nation's vision for the future.

Beyond Rwanda's borders, icyizere serves as an inspiration to the world. It stands as a testament to the indomitable human spirit, proving that even in the aftermath of the darkest chapters in history, hope can endure. Rwanda's story of resilience, guided by icyizere, underscores the universal truth that a brighter future is attainable through unity, compassion, and unwavering determination. It reminds us that hope is not only a guiding principle but a transformative force capable of healing societies, mending divisions, and forging a path towards lasting peace and prosperity.

In Rwandan culture, icyizere is not just a concept; it is a living testament to the human capacity for resilience and the unwavering belief in a brighter, more harmonious future, even in the face of unimaginable adversity.

CHAPTER 11: Letter to survivors

In the aftermath of the Genocide against Tutsi, a dark chapter in human history, there emerges a powerful narrative of resilience, strength, and hope. This chapter is dedicated to exploring the profound impact of writing letters of appreciation to the survivors of this horrific event. It delves into the transformative power of expressing gratitude, admiration, and support to those who have endured unspeakable atrocities and emerged as beacons of resilience.

Within these pages, we aim to shed light on the significance of acknowledging the strength and courage displayed by Genocide against Tutsi survivors. We delve into the act of writing letters of appreciation as a means of recognizing their journey and offering solace amidst unimaginable pain.

Each letter penned to a survivor serves as a testament to the indomitable human spirit. They bear witness to the stories of survival, resilience, and the unwavering commitment to rebuilding shattered lives and communities. The letters encapsulate the deep admiration and gratitude for the survivors' ability to rise above adversity and reclaim their lives, in spite of the indelible scars left by the Genocide.

Through heartfelt expressions of empathy, support, and encouragement, these letters aim to provide a ray of light in the lives of survivors. They serve as a reminder that their resilience is not only recognized but cherished by others. Moreover, they embody a collective commitment to standing by the survivors' side, amplifying their voices, and fostering healing, justice, and reconciliation.

This chapter invites readers to explore the art of writing letters of appreciation with sensitivity, respect, and deep reflection. It shares insights into the process of crafting heartfelt messages that honor the survivors' journey, validate their experiences, and inspire continued strength and growth.

Part I: Resilience for resilients

As we embark on this exploration, let us remember the tremendous responsibility we bear in engaging with this topic. The Genocide against Tutsi survivors have experienced profound trauma, and it is our duty to approach their stories and resilience with the utmost care and respect. By writing letters of appreciation, we contribute to a collective narrative of healing, empowerment, and hope in the face of unimaginable darkness.

May these letters be a testament to the enduring human spirit, and may they serve as a catalyst for continued support, understanding, and compassion towards Genocide against Tutsi survivors. Together, let us embrace the transformative power of expressing our heartfelt appreciation and contribute to the ongoing process of healing and resilience.

Through the act of writing these letters, we aim to create a space of compassion, validation, and support for the survivors. It is an opportunity to recognize their immense courage, honor their stories, and celebrate their resilience in the face of unimaginable adversity. By putting pen to paper and expressing our heartfelt appreciation, we offer a lifeline of empathy and understanding.

These letters of appreciation not only serve as a source of validation for the survivors but also provide an avenue for the writers to engage in meaningful reflection. They allow us to confront the profound impact of the Genocide against Tutsi and grapple with the complexities of human suffering and resilience. Through writing these letters, we connect with the survivors' experiences on a deeply personal level, fostering empathy and a sense of shared humanity.

May this chapter inspire and empower you to pen your own letters of appreciation, and may these heartfelt messages serve as a testament to the indomitable spirit of the survivors. Together, let us honor their resilience, promote healing, and contribute to a future rooted in justice, reconciliation, and compassion.

Part I: Resilience for resilients

Before we proceed further into the chapter, it is important to acknowledge that the letters of appreciation we discuss and showcase within this book may predominantly be in Kinyarwanda, the native language of the Genocide against Tutsi survivors. We sincerely apologize to readers who may not understand Kinyarwanda and thus may not be able to fully grasp the content of these letters.

We recognize the significance of language as a means of cultural expression, connection, and healing. It is through the use of one's native language that survivors can often best convey their experiences, emotions, and thoughts. Therefore, in our effort to honor and amplify the voices of Genocide against Tutsi survivors, it is fitting to include letters in Kinyarwanda.

While we acknowledge the language barrier that some readers may face, we encourage you to approach these letters with an open heart and an appreciation for the sentiment they convey. Although you may not understand the precise words, the emotions and intentions behind these letters transcend language barriers. They serve as a testament to the survivors' resilience, strength, and the deep gratitude expressed towards them.

We believe that the inclusion of these Kinyarwanda letters is vital to preserving the authenticity and cultural context of the Genocide against Tutsi survivors. It is an opportunity for readers to witness the power of language in capturing the essence of their experiences, while also acknowledging the limitations of translation.

We understand that the inability to understand the specific content of these letters may evoke feelings of exclusion or frustration. We apologize for any disappointment this may cause. However, we assure you that the broader themes and messages conveyed through these letters will be explored and discussed in subsequent sections of the book.

As we move forward in this chapter, we invite you to reflect on the universal aspects of resilience, appreciation, and compassion that transcend language barriers. We endeavor to provide a comprehensive understanding of the impact and significance of writing letters of appreciation to Genocide against Tutsi survivors, recognizing that these letters serve as a testament to their remarkable strength and unwavering spirit.

The letters of appreciation we will see in this chapter of this book are particularly significant because they are written by the children of Genocide against Tutsi survivors. These letters serve as a powerful symbol of transgenerational resilience and the enduring impact of the survivors' experiences on future generations.

As children of survivors, we have witnessed firsthand the strength, courage, and determination displayed by our parents and families in the aftermath of the Genocide. We have grown up with their stories of survival, their resilience in the face of unimaginable adversity, and their unwavering commitment to rebuilding their lives and communities.

Writing these letters is our way of acknowledging the profound impact that the Genocide against Tutsi has had on our lives. We have witnessed the intergenerational transmission of trauma, but we have also inherited the legacy of resilience and strength from our parents. Through these letters, we express our deep admiration and gratitude for their ability to persevere, heal, and create a better future for us.

Furthermore, these letters signify the important role that the younger generation plays in preserving the memory, honoring the resilience, and continuing the legacy of the survivors. We recognize the responsibility we have to carry their stories forward, to advocate for justice, and to ensure that the lessons learned from the past are never forgotten.

Writing these letters is not only a way for us to show appreciation to our parents and survivors, but it is also a means of personal healing and growth. It allows us to process our own emotions, reflect on the impact of the Genocide on our lives, and find strength in the resilience that has been passed down to us.

Part I: Resilience for resilients

These letters also serve as a bridge between the past and the future, connecting the experiences of the survivors to the aspirations of the next generation. They represent our commitment to continue the fight against hatred, discrimination, and injustice. We aim to build a world where such atrocities are never repeated, where resilience is celebrated, and where the voices of the survivors are amplified.

The letters of appreciation written by the children of Genocide against Tutsi survivors embody the transgenerational resilience and the enduring impact of the survivors' experiences on future generations. They are a testament to the strength, courage, and determination of our parents and families, and they represent our commitment to carrying their stories forward and creating a better future for all.

Part I: Resilience for resilients

To every Genocide against Tutsi survivor,

Words alone cannot fully capture the depth of appreciation and value we hold for each and every one of you. While letters serve as a means to express our gratitude, they can never fully encompass the magnitude of your resilience, strength, and the profound impact you have on the world.

We recognize that the Genocide against Tutsi survivors have endured unspeakable atrocities, faced unimaginable challenges, and carried the weight of immeasurable loss. Yet, despite the darkness you have faced, you have emerged as beacons of hope, embodying the indomitable spirit of survival.

Your experiences, your stories, and your resilience are a testament to the human capacity for strength and healing. We want you to know that you are deeply appreciated, valued, and cherished. Your presence in this world is a constant reminder of the power of the human spirit to overcome even the darkest of times.

Beyond the letters of appreciation, we strive to create a world where you feel heard, seen, and validated. We are committed to standing alongside you, advocating for justice, promoting healing, and fostering understanding. We want to ensure that your voices are amplified, that your stories are told with respect and accuracy, and that your experiences are recognized and remembered.

You are not alone in your journey. We, as a collective community, stand with you in solidarity, ready to offer support, empathy, and compassion. Your presence enriches our lives, inspires us to strive for a better world, and reminds us of the importance of resilience and hope.

We invite you to embrace your own worth, knowing that your resilience goes far beyond what any letter can express. Your existence is a testament to the strength of the human spirit, and we honor your journey of healing, growth, and transformation.

Part I: Resilience for resilients

Please know that you are appreciated and valued more than words can convey. We are committed to creating spaces where your experiences are acknowledged and celebrated. We pledge to continue working towards justice, healing, and reconciliation, knowing that your contributions to society are immeasurable.

With deepest gratitude and respect,
Akariza Laurette Annely.

Part I: Resilience for resilients

Dear Survivors,

It is important to acknowledge the immense pain you carry and the profound impact the Genocide has had on your lives. The scars, both physical and emotional, may never fully heal, but please know that you are not alone. The world stands with you in solidarity, offering support, understanding, and a commitment to justice.

Your stories and testimonies have shed light on the darkest corners of humanity, serving as a reminder of the consequences of prejudice, hatred, and indifference. Your courage in sharing your experiences has helped bring about awareness, education, and prevention efforts to ensure that such atrocities never occur again.

While the path to healing may be long and challenging, I urge you to continue seeking solace, strength, and support from one another. Your unity and determination to rebuild your lives and communities have been truly inspiring. Together, you have shown the world the power of forgiveness, reconciliation, and hope. It is our collective responsibility to remember the victims, honor their memory, and work tirelessly towards creating a world where such acts of violence and discrimination have no place. Let us stand together to advocate for justice, equality, and peace, not just for Rwanda, but for all humanity. May the memory of those lost in the Genocide against the Tutsi be a guiding light, reminding us of the urgent need to foster understanding, compassion, and respect among all people.

As we move forward, let us ensure that their lives were not lost in vain, but rather serve as a catalyst for positive change and a future marked by unity and harmony. With heartfelt condolences and unwavering support.

Marie Louise Murekatete

Part I: Resilience for resilients

Dear Survivors,

As a generation after the Genocide against Tutsis 1994, we can not fail to honor the survivors for their fortitude. We can not fully comprehend what it was like to live the life they've lived when they were our age, but we can only appreciate how they've strived to give us the life they've never had a chance to enjoy.

We learn from you every day dear parents/older brothers and sisters. From you we can learn that life is a gift from above and that fortitude creates character. We thank you for your courage in honoring those we've lost, and the effort put in fighting for the Truth to be known by us, for the sake of safeguarding our true History. We look up to you in a lot of things, in forgiveness, rebuilding oneself and indeed in you we can withdraw hope that even after the a long night, rays of the sun can be seen at the end of the tunnel. We pray that as we are still graced with your presence, we shall not grieve you and put to vain your efforts by becoming cowards, but will follow into your steps in putting our efforts into building our country in peace and Unity.

We will be True fruitful branches that came from a tree of suffering but yet through the nourishment of Hope and resilience, didn't wither nor droop. The future is bright through the hope we've seen in you. We love you and will always strive to heal the rest of your wounds.

We can not also forget to thank God who has left you for a reason and has given you the strength towards resilience and hopefulness. #TheFutureIsBright

Olave Quentin SHAMI

Kigali 19/6/2023
Kigali-Gasabo
Kacyiru

Kubashimira kubw'ubudaheranwa bwanyu nyuma yo kurokoka Jenoside yakorewe Abatutsi mu 1994.

Imyaka irenga 35 mutotezwa, mwicwa ndetse munahozwa ku nkeke cyari igihe kigoye ndetse cyo kwiyanga no kwiheba ariko mwakomeje kubaho n'ahatarabonekaga ubuzima, mwakomeje kurera abana banyu murabakorera, murabigisha aho batabashaga kwiga, Jenoside yaje ibasozerezaho ubuzima kuko bwari bumaze kuba buke nyuma y'igihe kirekire mutegurirwa kwicwa.

Kuva mu kibona Inkotanyi mwabonye ubuzima, mu gihe mwatekerezaga ko ubuzima burangiye mwongeye kugira ikizere cyo kubaho. Mwabuze ababyeyi, mwabuze abana, mwabuze abavandimwe, mwabuze abafasha, mubura inshuti, mubura abaturanyi gusa ntimwabuze igihugu.

Ndabashimira ko mwemeye gufatanya n'inkotanyi mukubaka igihugu, mukemere kubana n'ababiciye, mugatanga imbabazi no ku batarazibasabye kandi mwari imbabare, impano iruta izindi mwahaye iki gihugu. Mwiziritse umukanda, mukenyerera umukandara ku nkovu z'ibikomere bya Jenoside yakorewe Abatutsi mu 1994, mufata iya mbere mu kubaka u Rwanda mwaburiyemo amahoro mwe muba umusemburo wayo.

Ndabashimira ku bw'ubutwari, kwirenga, kwitsinda, ndetse n'ubudaheranwa bwintagereranywa mwagize kandi uranabikomeje.

Gukunda ighugu, kubabarira, kwitanga, kudatsimburwa no kugira intego ni umurage mwahaye iki gihugu.

Part I: Resilience for resilients

Gusigara uri wenyine mu muryango wari ufite uwufite, kubura abana bawe bose, kwicirwa umufasha n'abakagufashije bose ariko ugakomeza kugaba urukundo n'ineza ni umurage abato tuzasigasira, ni umuriro tuzahora twenyegeza, ni igicaniro kitazasinzira kandi ni itabaza ritubineshereza.

Wowe warokotse Jenoside yakorewe Abatutsi Impore, Shisha,Shinjagira niyo waba ushira, Hesha shema abawe ushobore mu buzima, Komera burya amakoma ava ahakomeye, Nubwo wakomeretse ariko turiho ngo tukomore, Nubwo watemwe warashibutse, Ntugipfuye kandi ufite ubuzima, Dadira, Hobera ubuzima,Jya mbere, twaza, utware, Ukwire, Ugare nk'umunyinya, Ugwize ubuzima buzima buzira kuzima kuko Inkotanyi zaguhaye ubuzima kandi abawe ntibazazima.

Twebwe amashami yashibutse dushishikariye kubabera icyomoro, kubabera urwibutso, kubabera igihozo, kusa ikivi cy'abacu aribo banyu bagiye batushije.

Ubuzima buriho, burashoboka, imbere ni heza kandi turakataje, Jenoside ntizongera ukundi mukomeze ugane imbere dukorere igihugu tuzakiture kandi turage abazadukomokaho igihugu cyiza.

Muhire Leon Pierre

CHAPTER 1: Beyond Survival: Thriving in the Wake of Genocide

"Beyond Survival: Thriving in the Wake of Genocide" is a concept that delves into the profound challenges faced by individuals and communities who have survived genocidal atrocities and explores their ability to not only endure but also flourish in the aftermath. It encompasses the resilience, strength, and determination that survivors exhibit as they strive to rebuild their lives, their communities, and their collective identities.

Surviving Genocide, which involves the systematic and intentional destruction of a particular ethnic, religious, or social group, is a harrowing ordeal that leaves deep physical, psychological, and emotional scars on survivors. Beyond Survival acknowledges the immense trauma and suffering that survivors endure and recognizes that merely surviving is not the end of their journey but rather the beginning of a complex process of healing and rebuilding.

One crucial aspect of thriving beyond survival is the process of healing. Genocides often lead to profound emotional and psychological trauma, as survivors witness and experience horrific acts of violence, loss of loved ones, and the destruction of their homes and communities. Healing involves not only addressing the immediate physical and mental health needs of survivors but also providing them with the tools and support necessary to cope with their trauma. This may include therapy, counseling, and the creation of safe spaces for survivors to share their stories and connect with others who have had similar experiences.

Beyond Survival also emphasizes the importance of justice and accountability. Holding perpetrators of Genocide accountable for their actions is a critical step in the healing process. It sends a message that such atrocities will not go unpunished and can help survivors find a sense of closure. Additionally, justice can play a role in preventing future Genocides by establishing a deterrent for potential perpetrators.

Rebuilding communities and restoring a sense of belonging is another central element of thriving beyond survival. Genocides often fracture communities, tearing apart the social fabric that held them together.

Rebuilding involves not only physical reconstruction but also the reestablishment of social bonds and trust among survivors. It may also include efforts to preserve cultural traditions and languages that were targeted during the Genocide.

Education plays a pivotal role in thriving beyond survival. Access to education can empower survivors to reclaim their agency, rebuild their lives, and contribute to their communities and societies. It can also help combat the ignorance and prejudice that often underlie genocidal ideologies.

"Beyond Survival: Thriving in the Wake of Genocide" encapsulates the resilience and determination of survivors to not only overcome the horrors of Genocide but also to heal, seek justice, rebuild their communities, and ultimately thrive. It highlights the importance of addressing the multifaceted needs of survivors and the broader societal responsibilities of preventing future Genocides and promoting reconciliation and healing. Beyond Survival serves as a testament to the indomitable human spirit and the potential for hope and renewal even in the darkest of circumstances.

CHAPTER 2: The Psychological Tapestry: Weaving Past, Present, and Future

The concept of the Psychological Tapestry provides a fascinating perspective on how our past, present, and future experiences are intricately woven together, influencing our thoughts, emotions, and actions. Imagine your life as a grand, vibrant quilt, with each patch representing a unique life event or experience. Some patches are remnants of the past, like childhood memories or significant life events. Others represent your current circumstances and the activities you engage in daily, while there are also patches symbolizing your hopes, dreams, and expectations for the future. As you weave these pieces together, they form a complex and beautiful tapestry, much like the intricate web of your mind.

In this metaphor, your past serves as the foundation of the tapestry. Past experiences and memories are like threads that have already been integrated into the fabric. They influence how you perceive the present and shape your emotional responses. For instance, a happy childhood can contribute to a more positive outlook on life, while past traumas may cast a shadow on your present emotions and behaviors.

The present moment is where the ongoing process of weaving takes place. Your current experiences, actions, and interactions are the threads being added to the tapestry in real-time. They affect your emotions, thoughts, and behaviors, just as your immediate surroundings and circumstances impact your mood and mindset. For instance, a stressful day at work can influence your overall mood and decision-making.

The future, represented by your hopes and aspirations, plays a crucial role in this tapestry. These aspirations are like threads you're preparing to weave into your life's fabric. Your goals, dreams, and plans can motivate your actions in the present, guiding your choices and behaviors. For instance, if you dream of becoming a doctor, your dedication to your studies and career path will be shaped by this vision.

What makes the Psychological Tapestry concept so profound is that it emphasizes the interconnectedness of these threads. Your past experiences mold your perceptions and responses in the present, while your current actions and emotions have the potential to influence your future experiences. It's a continuous and dynamic weaving process, where each thread contributes to the overall pattern of your life.

Understanding this psychological tapestry allows you to make sense of your emotions and behaviors. It empowers you to recognize how your past has shaped your present, and how your present choices can mold your future. By acknowledging these interconnections, you can work towards creating a more harmonious and fulfilling tapestry of life experiences.

In the Rwandan context, the idea of a psychological tapestry, which weaves together past, present, and future experiences, holds significant relevance. This concept can help shed light on the intricate complexities of Rwanda's history, its process of healing and reconciliation, and its aspirations for the future.

The threads of the past in Rwanda are deeply entwined with the traumatic events of the Genocide against the Tutsi 1994. The memories of this dark period continue to shape the present and influence the emotions, attitudes, and behaviors of Rwandans. Many individuals carry the heavy burden of personal losses and collective trauma. The psychological tapestry metaphor allows us to understand how these past experiences serve as a foundation for the present, impacting the thoughts and emotions of survivors, perpetrators, and their descendants.

Rwanda is characterized by ongoing efforts towards reconciliation and unity. The government's emphasis on a common Rwandan identity, transcending ethnic divisions, represents an endeavor to reweave the social fabric of the nation. However, the subtext of these efforts often involves unspoken tensions, complexities, and the delicate balance between acknowledging the past while forging a united future. The psychological tapestry concept helps us appreciate how these present-day dynamics are interwoven with the threads of history, shaping the nation's path towards healing and reconciliation.

Looking towards the future, Rwanda aspires to build a more inclusive and prosperous society. The threads of hope, dreams, and aspirations for a brighter tomorrow are being woven into the tapestry of the nation's collective psyche. These aspirations guide present actions and policies aimed at economic development, education, and social progress. By understanding this subtext of hope and ambition, one can gain insight into Rwanda's determination to overcome its painful past and create a more harmonious future.

Moreover, the idea of a psychological tapestry in the Rwandan context emphasizes the importance of acknowledging what is not said. Many Rwandans may choose not to openly discuss their experiences, emotions, or perspectives due to the sensitivity of topics like the Genocide. Recognizing the subtext and unspoken emotions allows for a more empathetic and supportive approach to those who carry the weight of Rwanda's history.

The psychological tapestry metaphor, when applied to Rwanda, offers a profound understanding of how the threads of the past, present, and future are interwoven in the nation's complex narrative. It highlights the enduring impact of history on the present, the delicate process of reconciliation and unity, and the unwavering hope for a brighter future. Recognizing the subtext within this tapestry allows us to engage with Rwanda's unique journey towards healing and progress with empathy and respect.

CHAPTER 3: Rebuilding Rwanda: From Ashes to Aspirations

In the tapestry of Rwanda's history, this chapter unfurls like a masterpiece, where the threads of tragedy are intricately woven into the fabric of resilience and rebirth. As we step into the heart of this narrative, we find ourselves standing at the intersection of sorrow and hope, where the human spirit, once tested to its limits, emerges triumphant against the darkest of backgrounds. In this chapter, Rwanda's canvas, once marred by the stains of a brutal Genocide, transforms into a vibrant tapestry of recovery, renewal, and redemption, each stroke of progress illuminating a path towards aspirations previously unimaginable.

Imagine a phoenix rising from the ashes, Rwanda, a nation reborn, defying the confines of despair to soar towards the heights of its potential. Here, we explore the intricate brushwork of transformation, revealing the layers of healing, the palette of reconciliation, and the vibrant hues of economic growth. Each paragraph is a stroke of the artist's brush, unveiling the complexities of this remarkable journey, where every detail tells a story of tragedy and triumph, of scars and resilience, and ultimately, of a nation's indomitable spirit. Welcome to the canvas of Rwanda's evolution, where the artistry of recovery is a testament to the limitless capacity of the human heart to paint over the darkest of pasts with the brightest of futures.

Rwanda's journey from the ashes of one of the darkest periods in human history to its aspirations of becoming a thriving, resilient nation is a testament to the indomitable human spirit and the power of effective governance. In the mid-1990s, Rwanda was torn apart by a brutal Genocide that claimed the lives of nearly a million people in just 100 days. The world watched in horror as this small African nation descended into chaos, but what followed was a remarkable story of resilience and transformation.

After the Genocide, Rwanda faced the daunting task of rebuilding its shattered society, economy, and infrastructure. The country's leadership, under President Paul Kagame, embarked on a path of reconciliation, justice, and nation-building. One of the most remarkable aspects of Rwanda's recovery has been its emphasis on unity and healing. The government initiated Gacaca courts, a traditional justice system, to address the crimes committed during the Genocide. This innovative approach allowed communities to participate in the process of justice, fostering a sense of ownership in the healing process.

Economically, Rwanda has made significant strides as well. It has become one of Africa's fastest-growing economies, with an impressive average annual growth rate. The government has focused on diversifying the economy, investing in infrastructure, and promoting business-friendly policies. The country has attracted foreign investment and established itself as a hub for technology and innovation on the continent, earning the nickname "Africa's Singapore."

Furthermore, Rwanda's commitment to education has been instrumental in its transformation. The government has prioritized education as a means to break the cycle of poverty and ensure a brighter future for its citizens. Investments in education have led to a significant increase in literacy rates and access to quality healthcare, contributing to improved living standards.

In the realm of governance, Rwanda has made strides in combating corruption and promoting transparency. It ranks among the least corrupt countries in Africa, a testament to its commitment to good governance. The gender balance in political leadership is another remarkable achievement, with Rwanda boasting one of the highest percentages of women in parliament globally.

Rwanda's aspirations extend beyond its borders, as it plays an active role in regional and international affairs. The nation has contributed troops to United Nations peacekeeping missions, showcasing its commitment to global stability and peace. Moreover, it has hosted several high-profile international conferences and summits, further solidifying its position on the global stage.

Rwanda's transformation from the horrors of Genocide to its current aspirations as a thriving nation is a multifaceted story. One of the cornerstones of this transformation has been the commitment to national reconciliation. In the aftermath of the Genocide, the Rwandan government initiated extensive programs to facilitate dialogue and healing between survivors and perpetrators. This challenging process, while painful, played a vital role in rebuilding trust and fostering unity among Rwandans. It demonstrated that Rwanda was not only rebuilding its physical infrastructure but also the social fabric of the nation, emphasizing the importance of forgiveness and reconciliation in the face of unspeakable tragedy.

Youth empowerment has been another critical component of Rwanda's resurgence. Recognizing that the country's young population is the key to its future, Rwanda has invested heavily in programs like YouthConnekt. These initiatives aim to equip young Rwandans with skills, education, and opportunities for personal and professional development. By doing so, Rwanda reduces the risk of radicalization and promotes social cohesion among its youth, ensuring that they play a central role in shaping the nation's future.

Environmental sustainability is a priority for Rwanda. The country has not only protected its unique biodiversity but has also leveraged it for eco-tourism. Its commitment to conservation has positioned Rwanda as a leader in the fight against climate change and plastic pollution. Bans on single-use plastics and investments in renewable energy showcase Rwanda's dedication to a greener future, aligning its aspirations with global environmental goals.

Infrastructure development has been crucial for Rwanda's economic growth. Investments in roads, bridges, and airports have facilitated trade and connectivity within the region. Rwanda's strategic location has allowed it to become a logistics hub, attracting businesses and investments that further fuel its economic progress. These infrastructure developments have paved the way for a more prosperous and connected Rwanda.

Healthcare advancements have significantly improved the well-being of Rwandans. The government has partnered with organizations like Partners In Health to enhance healthcare access for all citizens. Community health workers have played a pivotal role in delivering healthcare services, improving outcomes, and preventing diseases. These investments in healthcare underscore Rwanda's commitment to the welfare of its people.

Agricultural transformation remains a central focus of Rwanda's economic strategy. By modernizing the agricultural sector and promoting crop diversification, Rwanda has increased food security and reduced reliance on subsistence farming. Supporting smallholder farmers has been instrumental in driving rural development and poverty reduction.

Cultural preservation is another aspect of Rwanda's identity that the government has sought to protect. The preservation of traditional music, dance, art, and the Kinyarwanda language is an essential part of Rwanda's history and cultural heritage. These efforts ensure that Rwanda's unique identity continues to thrive in the face of modernization.

Investment in technology has positioned Rwanda as a tech-savvy nation. Initiatives like the "One Laptop Per Child" program have boosted digital literacy among the younger population, preparing them for the demands of the modern global economy. Rwanda's embrace of technology reflects its commitment to progress and innovation.

Tourism and conservation efforts have not only contributed to economic growth but have also raised awareness about Rwanda globally. The country's breathtaking landscapes, including the Virunga Mountains, are home to a significant population of mountain gorillas. Tourism revenue has played a vital role in both protecting these endangered animals and boosting the nation's economy, demonstrating that conservation and economic development can go hand in hand.

Education has been a cornerstone of Rwanda's resurgence. The government has undertaken comprehensive reforms to improve access to quality education at all levels. The establishment of the 9-12-12 education system, which ensures nine years of basic education, followed by a 3-year lower secondary cycle, and a 2-year upper secondary cycle, has laid the foundation for a more educated and skilled workforce. Scholarships and incentives for teachers have also played a crucial role in raising educational standards, contributing to improved human capital.

In the realm of governance, Rwanda has implemented innovative solutions to combat corruption and promote transparency. One standout initiative is the use of technology in public service delivery. The introduction of the "Irembo" platform, an e-government portal, has streamlined government services, reducing opportunities for corruption and enhancing efficiency. Additionally, the Ombudsman's office has played a pivotal role in addressing citizen complaints and ensuring accountability in public administration.

Rwanda's commitment to gender equality is a beacon of progress. The nation has made substantial strides in promoting women's rights and participation in all sectors of society. The landmark achievement of having one of the highest percentages of women in parliament globally showcases Rwanda's dedication to gender balance in political leadership. Women also play a significant role in the workforce, contributing to economic growth and development.

Entrepreneurship and innovation have flourished in Rwanda. The government's support for startups and small and medium-sized enterprises (SMEs) has fostered a vibrant entrepreneurial ecosystem. Initiatives like the Kigali Innovation City, a technology and business hub, provide a platform for creativity and innovation, attracting both domestic and foreign investment.

Rwanda's commitment to peace and security extends beyond its borders. The nation has been actively involved in United Nations peacekeeping missions, contributing troops to various conflict zones. This participation not only reflects Rwanda's dedication to global stability but also strengthens its international partnerships and diplomacy efforts.

Infrastructure development has not been limited to physical infrastructure. Rwanda has also invested in digital infrastructure, expanding internet connectivity and digital literacy. This digital transformation has not only improved access to information but has also facilitated e-commerce and the growth of the technology sector.

In terms of regional integration, Rwanda is a member of the East African Community (EAC), a regional economic bloc that promotes cooperation and trade among its member states. This partnership has opened up opportunities for cross-border trade and investment, further boosting Rwanda's economic prospects.

Rwanda's commitment to social welfare is evident in its efforts to provide social protection to vulnerable populations. Initiatives like the Girinka program, which provides cows to poor households, have not only improved nutrition but have also contributed to poverty reduction and economic empowerment.

Diaspora Engagement:
Rwanda has made deliberate efforts to engage its diaspora community, often referred to as the "Sixth Region." Rwandans living abroad have been encouraged to invest in their homeland, both financially and through the transfer of skills and knowledge. This engagement has played a vital role in the country's development, with the diaspora contributing to various sectors such as business, education, and healthcare. Beyond economic contributions, the engagement of the diaspora has fostered a sense of connection and shared responsibility among Rwandans worldwide, strengthening the nation's global network of support.

Justice and Accountability:
The pursuit of justice and accountability for the Genocide has been a central and challenging endeavor in Rwanda's transformation. The International Criminal Tribunal for Rwanda (ICTR) played a pivotal role in prosecuting high-level perpetrators of the Genocide. Additionally, Rwanda's approach to justice at the community level through Gacaca courts, though unconventional, aimed to involve local communities in the

process of truth-telling and reconciliation. While these efforts have been commendable, they have also faced criticisms and complexities, demonstrating the difficulties of reconciling justice with healing in the aftermath of such a profound tragedy.

Media and Freedom of Expression:

Rwanda has made strides in developing a responsible and free media landscape. However, concerns have arisen regarding press freedom and the restriction of certain narratives. Balancing the need for open dialogue and the preservation of social cohesion has been an ongoing challenge in Rwanda's media environment. Striking the right balance between promoting free expression and maintaining a peaceful and stable society is a complex task that Rwanda continues to grapple with as it seeks to nurture a vibrant and informed public discourse.

Challenges in Reconciliation:

Despite commendable efforts at reconciliation, Rwanda still faces significant challenges in achieving full healing and reconciliation. Many survivors continue to grapple with profound trauma, and the journey toward reintegration and forgiveness remains deeply personal and often difficult. Achieving a sense of closure and lasting reconciliation for all Rwandans remains an ongoing and deeply human process.

Economic Disparities:

While Rwanda's economic progress has been substantial, economic disparities persist within the country. Some regions and communities continue to experience disparities in wealth and living standards. The government has implemented targeted development programs and poverty reduction initiatives to address these inequalities. The goal is to ensure that the benefits of economic growth are felt by all Rwandans and that no one is left behind in the journey toward prosperity.

Land Reforms:

Land issues have posed a significant challenge in Rwanda, given its high population density and competing land claims. The government has undertaken land reforms to address land tenure issues, mitigate conflicts, and ensure equitable access to land resources. These reforms are essential for both economic development and social stability, but their implementation has been complex and multifaceted.

Regional Relations:

Rwanda's role in the Great Lakes region of Africa has been influential yet complex. The nation has faced regional tensions and conflicts, especially with neighboring countries such as the Democratic Republic of Congo. Managing these diplomatic challenges while pursuing its national interests has required adept diplomacy and cooperation with regional partners.

Youth Employment:

Despite various youth empowerment initiatives, unemployment remains a concern in Rwanda, particularly among young Rwandans entering the job market. Bridging the gap between education and employment opportunities remains a challenge for the government, which continues to explore strategies to provide meaningful and sustainable employment for its youth population.

In conclusion, Rwanda's journey from devastation to hope is marked by its multifaceted approach to post-Genocide recovery and development. These additional aspects, including diaspora engagement, justice and accountability, media freedom, reconciliation challenges, economic disparities, land reforms, regional relations, and youth employment, demonstrate the complexities and ongoing nature of Rwanda's transformation. The nation's commitment to addressing these challenges is a testament to its resilience and determination in building a more inclusive and prosperous future for all Rwandans.

I am sitting here in 2023, and I stand here on the precipice of a new era, having witnessed three decades of rebirth, resilience, and recovery. The canvas of Rwanda's transformation, once stained with the indelible marks of tragedy, now radiates with the vibrancy of hope and possibility.

As I look ahead, I hold in our hearts the belief that Rwanda's story is far from complete. The masterpiece we've explored in these paragraphs is but a glimpse of the nation's potential. I eagerly await the forthcoming chapters, knowing that the artistic spirit of Rwanda will continue to evolve, enriching its tapestry with new colors of progress and new strokes of achievement.

In 2053, as Rwanda celebrates the 60th anniversary of its rebirth, we can only imagine the heights it will have reached, the innovations it will have pioneered, and the aspirations it will have realized. We leave this chapter behind with gratitude for the opportunity to witness and celebrate Rwanda's transformation, and with the unwavering belief that the best is yet to come. In 2023, we look forward to the next 30 years of Rwanda's journey with hope, excitement, and the expectation of even greater achievements on the horizon.

CHAPTER 4: Legacies of Strength: Stories from the Heart of Rwanda

"Legacies of strength" is a phrase that encapsulates the enduring impact of resilience, fortitude, and determination in the face of adversity. These legacies are often born out of challenging circumstances and serve as a testament to the human spirit's ability to triumph over obstacles. They leave behind a profound and lasting influence on individuals, communities, and even entire nations.

At its core, legacies of strength represent stories of individuals or groups who have faced extraordinary challenges, such as adversity, trauma, or crisis, and have emerged from these experiences with a newfound sense of purpose, resilience, and wisdom. These legacies can take various forms, ranging from personal narratives of survival and personal growth to broader societal transformations and cultural shifts.

Legacies of strength can inspire and uplift others, serving as a source of hope and motivation. They remind us that even in the most challenging circumstances, human beings can find the inner strength and determination to overcome, heal, and rebuild. These legacies also underscore the importance of compassion, unity, and the enduring human capacity for forgiveness and reconciliation.

In essence, legacies of strength are stories of human triumph in the face of adversity, and they continue to shape the way we perceive resilience, courage, and the limitless potential of the human spirit.

In the heart of Rwanda today, a remarkable story of resilience unfolds in real time, shaping the lives of its people in the most remarkable ways.

Here in this vibrant land, the spirit of resilience is not something of the past but a living, breathing force. People gather to dance to the rhythms of their ancestors, turning tradition into a celebration of their enduring spirit. With every step, they weave a colorful tapestry of culture, ensuring that the songs of their heritage echo through the present and into the future. It's not just about preserving history; it's about living it, making resilience an integral part of their daily lives.

Part II: Land of a Thousand Resilient Hills

In the close-knit communities, neighbors are like family, and their bonds are unbreakable. It's like an intricate web, a safety net of unity that catches those in need, ensuring that no one is left behind. Here, resilience is not just a word but a shared spirit that holds the community together, allowing them to weather any storm.

Amidst the bustling marketplaces, innovation is a vibrant force. Challenges are not obstacles but sparks that ignite the flames of creativity. Ingenious solutions to everyday problems and the birth of new businesses are the hallmarks of Rwanda's resilience. It's about transforming adversity into opportunity in the present moment, a continuous spark of creativity lighting up their path forward.

Yet, resilience isn't just about physical solutions; it's also about emotional healing. Rwandans have faced profound emotional wounds, but they don't let their hearts remain shattered. In the present, they gather the pieces, crafting a beautiful mosaic of recovery. Through sharing stories, seeking support, and extending forgiveness, they demonstrate that emotional resilience is an ongoing journey of transformation.

At the heart of this narrative are leaders who embody resilience in the present. They're not distant figures but active participants in the nation's journey. Picture leaders who work alongside their people, inspiring them to rise above adversity in real-time. Their leadership is a testament to the fact that resilience is not just a concept but a daily practice that echoes through the nation.

This story transcends borders; it reaches far beyond Rwanda's boundaries. Resilience here is not insular but expansive, like a bridge connecting them to the world. Rwanda is a global ambassador, contributing to peacekeeping missions, championing environmental causes, and extending a hand in times of humanitarian crises. In the present, their resilience is a reminder of the importance of global collaboration in overcoming shared challenges.

So, in the present moment, the story of Rwanda's resilience is not just a tale of survival but an ongoing epic of thriving. Culture, community, innovation, emotional strength, leadership, and global citizenship come together to paint a portrait of a nation that doesn't just endure but finds beauty and inspiration in the most unexpected places. It's a story that resonates across the world, reminding us all that resilience is not just a historical concept; it's a way of life in the here and now.

CHAPTER 5: Rwanda's New Dawn: Moving Forward without Forgetting

"Rwanda's New Dawn: Moving Forward without Forgetting" encapsulates the nation's remarkable journey of resilience and recovery following the horrific Genocide against the Tutsi This phrase signifies a profound commitment to rebuilding and progress while simultaneously acknowledging the painful history that still lingers in the collective memory of the Rwandan people.

At its core, this phrase speaks to the resilience of the Rwandan nation. In 1994, Rwanda experienced one of the most brutal episodes of ethnic violence in modern history, resulting in the loss of nearly a million lives in just a few months. The aftermath left Rwanda in ruins, both physically and emotionally. However, rather than succumbing to despair, Rwanda chose resilience. The determination to move forward, rebuild, and ensure a better future for its citizens is a testament to the strength of the Rwandan people.

Resilience, in the context of Rwanda, is not simply about bouncing back from adversity; it's about healing and reconciliation. The phrase "Moving Forward without Forgetting" emphasizes the critical need to address the deep wounds and divisions that the Genocide left behind. Rwanda has employed various strategies to promote national healing and reconciliation. The establishment of the Gacaca courts, for example, allowed communities to seek justice at a local level, encouraging truth-telling, forgiveness, and the restoration of trust among neighbors.

Moreover, "Moving Forward without Forgetting" underscores the importance of acknowledging the past while working toward a brighter future. Rwanda is determined not to forget the horrors of the Genocide, not to perpetuate hatred, but to learn from the past to ensure that such atrocities never occur again. By remembering and commemorating the victims, Rwanda sends a powerful message to the world about the consequences of ethnic hatred and the imperative of preventing Genocides elsewhere.

Part II: Land of a Thousand Resilient Hills

The resilience of Rwanda is also evident in its commitment to building a more inclusive society. The Genocide was marked by deep ethnic divisions between the Hutu and Tutsi communities. "Rwanda's New Dawn" signifies a determination to transcend these divisions and promote a shared national identity. The emphasis on Rwandan unity and identity has been instrumental in reducing ethnic tensions and fostering social cohesion.

Economically, Rwanda has demonstrated resilience by achieving significant growth and development. Despite the devastation of the Genocide, the nation has implemented visionary development plans like Vision 2020, focusing on economic diversification, infrastructure development, and attracting foreign investment. This economic resilience not only uplifts the lives of Rwandans but also reduces the vulnerabilities that could lead to future conflicts.

Internationally, Rwanda's commitment to "Moving Forward without Forgetting" extends beyond its borders. The nation actively participates in global efforts to prevent Genocide and mass atrocities. Rwandan leaders, including President Paul Kagame, have become vocal advocates for global peace and conflict prevention. Rwanda's resilience serves as an inspiring example of how a nation can lead by example and contribute to international peace and security.

"Rwanda's New Dawn: Moving Forward without Forgetting" represents the indomitable spirit of a nation that has endured unspeakable tragedy and emerged stronger. It symbolizes Rwanda's commitment to healing, reconciliation, economic progress, and global peace. This phrase reminds us all of the importance of acknowledging history and working tirelessly to create a more peaceful and just world, where resilience and hope triumph over the darkest of times.

Certainly, let's explore the deeper layers of "Rwanda's New Dawn: Moving Forward without Forgetting" in separate paragraphs:

Unseen Emotional Scars: Beyond the surface narrative of resilience, the phrase doesn't fully convey the profound emotional scars that linger in the hearts and minds of Rwandans. The Genocide against the Tutsi left a legacy of unimaginable grief and trauma, with many survivors struggling to cope with the psychological wounds that persist to this day. The phrase does not explicitly acknowledge the emotional resilience of individuals who have had to rebuild their lives while carrying the weight of their personal losses and traumatic memories.

Silent Role of International Support: While celebrating Rwanda's determination to rebuild, it often goes unsaid that international support played an instrumental role in the nation's recovery. Humanitarian aid, peacekeeping missions, and diplomatic efforts from the global community were pivotal in stabilizing the country in the aftermath of the Genocide. Recognizing this international solidarity is essential to comprehending the full scope of Rwanda's resilience journey.

Complexities of Pursuing Justice: Rwanda's commitment to justice for the perpetrators of the Genocide is a multifaceted process that the phrase doesn't delve into. Striking a balance between accountability and reconciliation is a delicate challenge. The phrase doesn't explore the intricacies and difficulties faced in holding individuals accountable for their roles in the Genocide while simultaneously promoting national healing and unity.

Nuanced Societal Reintegration: The phrase doesn't explicitly touch upon the nuanced process of reintegrating individuals who were involved in the Genocide back into Rwandan society. Efforts to rehabilitate and reintegrate former combatants, acknowledging their wrongdoing while providing them with opportunities to rebuild their lives, involve complex dynamics and tensions that remain largely unspoken.

The Unsung Role of Youth: Rwanda's younger generation, often referred to as the "post-Genocide generation," has been a driving force behind the nation's resilience. While the phrase lauds Rwanda's recovery, it doesn't emphasize the active engagement of Rwandan youth in initiatives aimed at promoting unity, peace, and reconciliation. Their dedication to learning from the past and shaping a brighter future deserves more recognition.

Challenges in Commemoration: Rwanda's commitment to remembering the Genocide includes annual memorial ceremonies and the establishment of Genocide memorials. However, the phrase doesn't delve into the challenges and sensitivities surrounding commemoration, especially among different ethnic groups. The process of memorialization and its impact on various segments of society remain complex and often unspoken.

The Role of Women: Women in Rwanda have played an essential yet often uncelebrated role in the nation's recovery and resilience. They have been active participants in reconciliation initiatives, peacebuilding efforts, and community development. Recognizing and appreciating the contributions of women in rebuilding Rwanda is essential to understanding the complete narrative of the nation's journey.

Environmental Resilience: Another layer of resilience not highlighted in the phrase is Rwanda's commitment to sustainable development and environmental conservation. The nation has taken proactive steps to protect its natural resources, combat deforestation, and address climate change. This commitment to environmental sustainability contributes to long-term resilience, ensuring a stable ecosystem and resource base even in the face of environmental challenges.

"Rwanda's New Dawn: Moving Forward without Forgetting" represents a powerful narrative of resilience, but beneath the surface, there are countless untold stories, complexities, and ongoing challenges that shape Rwanda's journey. The emotional scars, international support, justice complexities, societal reintegration, youth involvement, commemoration challenges, the role of women, and environmental resilience all contribute to the multifaceted and inspiring story of Rwanda's recovery and progress.

CHAPTER 6: Children of Hope: The Next Generation's Vision for Rwanda

Rwanda's history is deeply marked by the Genocide that occurred in 1994, leaving a painful legacy of loss and trauma. In the aftermath of this tragedy, Rwanda embarked on a remarkable journey of healing, reconciliation, and nation-building. Central to this journey is the perspective of the young generation who have come of age in a nation that is actively working to overcome its traumatic past. "Children of Hope" is a term that encapsulates the spirit of resilience and optimism embodied by these young Rwandans.

As a young Rwandan, I am a part of the "Children of Hope" generation, and my vision for Rwanda is deeply rooted in the history and the experiences that have shaped me. Growing up in the aftermath of the Genocide against the Tutsi 1994, I have witnessed the resilience of my fellow Rwandans, the strength of our collective spirit, and the unwavering commitment to reconciliation.

Reconciliation and unity are at the core of my vision for Rwanda. I have seen the devastating consequences of division and conflict, and I believe that our nation's future depends on our ability to come together as one people. My generation understands the importance of promoting dialogue, forgiveness, and understanding among different ethnic groups. We envision a Rwanda where the scars of the past serve as a reminder of the need for unity, and we are determined to ensure that such a tragedy never happens again.

Education is a powerful tool for change, and it is central to my vision. Rwanda has made significant investments in education, and I see this as a pathway to a brighter future. I envision a Rwanda where every young person has access to quality education and the opportunity to develop their skills and talents. I want to see our nation become a hub of innovation and entrepreneurship, where young Rwandans are at the forefront of technological advancements and economic growth

Empowering the youth is essential for realizing our vision. We are the future leaders, and I believe that we should have a voice in shaping the policies and decisions that will impact our lives. I am passionate about initiatives that provide young Rwandans with the skills, knowledge, and opportunities needed to lead our country forward.

The significance of "Children of Hope" lies in its potential to inspire positive change and progress. These young Rwandans are not only shaping their own destinies but also contributing to Rwanda's broader goals of healing and development. Their commitment to reconciliation is essential for maintaining peace and unity, ensuring that the lessons of history are never forgotten.

Moreover, Rwanda's journey from a nation torn apart by conflict and Genocide to one working diligently towards unity and progress is a compelling story with global relevance. The world can draw inspiration from Rwanda's resilience, determination, and commitment to a brighter future.

The youth of Rwanda, in our vision, we see a nation where diversity is celebrated, where the scars of the past are healed through reconciliation, and where unity is not just a word but a way of life. we imagine a Rwanda where gender equality flourishes, empowering every girl and boy to reach their full potential, breaking down barriers that limit their ambitions.

These young visionaries are determined to create a Rwanda that is sustainable and environmentally conscious, where the lush landscapes are preserved for future generations. We dream of a Rwanda that harnesses the power of technology to drive economic growth, create jobs, and open up new opportunities for its citizens.

But our vision is not confined to our dreams alone; it is a call to action. The youth of Rwanda are willing to roll up our sleeves and work tirelessly to bring this vision to life. We understand that change starts with them, and we are committed to building bridges, fostering collaboration, and breaking down the walls that stand in the way of progress.

We are the Children of Hope, and we are ready to make it true. With determination, innovation, and a spirit of unity, we will work hand in hand with their fellow Rwandans to transform their nation into a place of boundless opportunity, where the dreams of today become the reality of tomorrow.

Our vision for Rwanda is not just a dream; it's a promise, a commitment, and a testament to the enduring spirit of a generation that believes in the power of hope, hard work, and the unwavering belief that a brighter future is within reach. Together, we will write the next chapter in Rwanda's history, a chapter filled with hope, progress, and the boundless potential of its youth.

CHAPTER 7: Lessons in Resilience: From Rwanda to the World

In the shadow of the Genocide against the Tutsi, where unspeakable horrors took place just three decades ago, a remarkable story of resilience emerged. Today, it stands as a testament to the indomitable human spirit and serves as an inspiring beacon of hope for the world.

It has been 30 years since that dark chapter in history unfolded, and the wounds remain fresh in the collective memory of a nation. For those born in the aftermath of the Genocide against the Tutsi, like myself, it might seem like a distant past, but the echoes of that tragedy still resonate with us. Our lives bear witness to the unimaginable strength that resides in the heart of every survivor.

The world, too, carries a debt—a debt to learn from the lessons of Rwandan resilience. It is a story of unity, forgiveness, and the unwavering commitment to rebuild when hope seemed lost. In the face of adversity and despair, Rwandans rose from the ashes, rebuilding their nation and their lives. This journey proves that even when the world turns a blind eye and hope dwindles, there is an undeniable capacity to rise, to heal, and to love again.

As we reflect on the enduring legacy of Rwandan resilience, it is our duty to share these profound lessons with the world. The resilience of a nation that refused to be defined by its darkest hour stands as an enduring source of inspiration and a reminder that even in the bleakest of times, the human spirit can rise and shine. These lessons are a beacon, guiding us towards a brighter and more compassionate future, where unity, forgiveness, and hope can prevail over hatred and division.

In sharing the lessons of Rwandan resilience with the world, I've chosen to utilize quotes.

Unity Prevails: "In unity, we discover our true strength, the power to overcome even the most daunting challenges."

The concept of unity is a fundamental lesson drawn from the resilience of Rwanda. In the wake of the Genocide against the Tutsi, where neighbor turned against neighbor, and a nation was torn apart by ethnic strife, the importance of unity became unmistakably clear. Rwandans, regardless of their backgrounds, were faced with the enormous task of rebuilding a nation fractured by hatred and violence. In this context, unity emerged as the cornerstone of their recovery.

The quote emphasizes that unity is not just a rallying cry or a hopeful aspiration; it's an unshakable truth. When people come together, their collective strength multiplies exponentially. Unity empowers individuals to transcend their individual limitations and work toward a common goal. In the case of Rwanda, this unity wasn't born from the absence of differences, but from the conscious choice to bridge those differences, to heal wounds, and to move forward together.

The power of unity, as demonstrated in Rwanda's journey, allowed them to confront the most daunting of challenges. It's what enabled the nation to rebuild in the face of staggering adversity. The unity of Rwandans served as the foundation upon which they could rebuild their communities, reconcile with one another, and forge a path toward a more peaceful and hopeful future.

This lesson teaches us that, no matter how insurmountable a challenge may appear, unity has the potential to turn the tide. It underscores the idea that when individuals and communities stand together, they can overcome obstacles that might seem impossible when faced alone. Unity is not only a source of strength; it's a guiding principle, a reminder that the power to effect positive change lies in our ability to unite, overcome divisions, and work collaboratively toward a better future.

Forgiveness Heals: "Forgiveness is the path to healing. It liberates us from the shackles of hatred."

The concept of forgiveness is a cornerstone of the Rwandan resilience narrative, and this quote beautifully encapsulates its significance. In the aftermath of one of the most devastating Genocides in history, Rwandans were left with wounds that ran deep, both individually and collectively. The need for forgiveness was not just a moral imperative but a pragmatic one if the nation was to move forward.

The quote underscores the profound transformative power of forgiveness. It's not merely an act of mercy but a path to personal and collective healing. When we forgive, we unburden ourselves from the weight of anger, bitterness, and the desire for vengeance. It's a liberating force that frees us from the shackles of hatred, which, if left unchecked, can perpetuate a cycle of violence and suffering.

Rwanda's journey is a testament to the fact that forgiveness is not a sign of weakness but an act of extraordinary strength. It requires tremendous courage to let go of the pain and anger caused by horrific atrocities. By choosing to forgive, individuals and communities chart a course towards reconciliation, peace, and a brighter future.

This lesson teaches us that forgiveness is not just a virtue; it's a practical and transformative force. It enables individuals to find closure, rebuild their lives, and engage with those they once considered enemies. On a broader scale, it paves the way for reconciliation and the mending of societal divisions.

In a world often marred by conflicts and grievances, the lesson of forgiveness from Rwandan resilience reminds us that the path to healing begins with the liberating act of forgiveness. It's an invitation to transcend hatred and find the strength to rebuild relationships, communities, and nations on the foundation of forgiveness and reconciliation.

Hope Lights the Way: "Even in the darkest times, hope is a beacon that can guide a nation forward."

This quote beautifully encapsulates the essence of hope in the context of Rwandan resilience. The Genocide against the Tutsi was a period of unspeakable darkness, where neighbors turned against neighbors and a nation was torn apart by violence and hatred. In the midst of this unimaginable tragedy, hope emerged as a vital force, offering a glimmer of light in the darkest of times.

The quote's message is both profound and universally resonant. It reminds us that even in the bleakest circumstances, hope is not extinguished. Instead, it serves as a guiding light, a source of inspiration, and a testament to the resilience of the human spirit. Hope is that unwavering belief that a better future is possible, no matter how dire the present may seem.

For Rwanda, hope was the beacon that guided them forward. It was the belief in the possibility of healing, reconciliation, and rebuilding. In a landscape scarred by loss and trauma, hope was the foundation upon which a shattered nation could start anew. It inspired individuals and communities to come together and work towards a future marked by peace and unity.

The lesson of hope is not limited to Rwanda; it is a universal truth. In times of personal adversity or global crises, hope can be the driving force that propels us forward. It ignites the human spirit, encourages perseverance, and fuels the determination to overcome challenges.

This lesson from Rwandan resilience reminds us that hope is not a passive wish but an active force for change. It calls on us to foster hope in ourselves and in others, recognizing that even in the darkest of times, it is hope that can ultimately guide us towards a brighter, more promising future. Hope is the beacon that leads us out of the darkest of tunnels, reminding us that, as long as there is hope, there is a path forward.

Diversity Empowers: "Our diversity is a source of strength; in our differences, we find unity."

This quote beautifully underscores the transformative power of embracing diversity, a crucial lesson derived from the Rwandan resilience story. In the aftermath of the Genocide against the Tutsi, where ethnic divisions had played a devastating role, Rwanda faced the immense challenge of reconciling a nation deeply scarred by hatred. The lesson that emerged is that diversity, far from being a source of division, is a wellspring of strength.

The quote's message reminds us that the very qualities that make us distinct, whether in terms of ethnicity, culture, or background, have the potential to unite us. It's a testament to the fact that diversity, when celebrated and harnessed, enriches the human experience and strengthens the bonds of community. Our differences, rather than being points of division, become sources of resilience and unity.

In Rwanda's case, embracing diversity was a conscious choice made by a nation determined to heal and rebuild. Instead of allowing divisions to persist, Rwandans recognized that their diversity could be a source of strength. Communities that were once divided came together, recognizing that unity in diversity could create a more robust and inclusive society.

This lesson extends far beyond the borders of Rwanda. It serves as a universal reminder that diversity is not a challenge to be overcome but an asset to be cherished. In a world marked by varying perspectives, backgrounds, and experiences, embracing diversity can foster understanding and cooperation. It is a lesson that calls on us to see our differences not as barriers but as bridges that lead to greater resilience and collective progress.

This quote serves as an inspiring invitation to celebrate and appreciate diversity, recognizing that it is through our differences that we can find common ground and forge a path to unity. In embracing diversity, we discover that our collective strength is immeasurable, and our capacity for resilience is boundless.

Rebuilding from Ashes: "Rebuilding is not just a possibility; it's our commitment, no matter how dire the circumstances."

This quote embodies the unwavering spirit of resilience that emerged from the heart of Rwanda. In the aftermath of the Genocide against the Tutsi, the nation faced a landscape of unimaginable destruction and suffering. Yet, this quote encapsulates the resolve of the Rwandan people: rebuilding was not merely a possibility; it was an unwavering commitment, an unshakable determination to rise from the ashes.

The quote serves as a powerful testament to human perseverance and the refusal to be defined by past atrocities. It reflects the collective commitment to healing and progress, even when circumstances seemed overwhelmingly dire. It is a declaration that no matter how devastating the challenges, the human spirit possesses the capacity to rebuild and emerge stronger than ever. In the context of Rwanda, this commitment to rebuilding was not an abstract concept. It involved the physical reconstruction of homes, communities, and infrastructure, but it went far beyond that. It encompassed the rebuilding of trust, the reconciliation of divided communities, and the restoration of hope. It was a commitment to forging a brighter future, rooted in the belief that a more peaceful, united, and resilient nation could emerge from the ruins.

The lesson conveyed in this quote extends far beyond Rwanda. It reminds us that even in the face of the most daunting challenges—whether on a personal or societal level—commitment and determination are the cornerstones of resilience. It is a call to action, urging us to acknowledge that, in the wake of any crisis, the commitment to rebuild and to strive for a better future is not just a possibility; it is a profound and unwavering commitment. This quote serves as an inspiration for all of us, emphasizing that when faced with seemingly insurmountable challenges, our determination and commitment can lead us to rebuild, heal, and ultimately, thrive. It is a powerful reminder that resilience is not only about bouncing back; it's about forging ahead with a renewed sense of purpose and a steadfast commitment to building a brighter future.

Trust Renewed: "Rebuilding trust is challenging but crucial for healing and progress."

This quote encapsulates a fundamental lesson from Rwanda's journey of resilience - the arduous yet indispensable process of rebuilding trust. In the wake of the Genocide against the Tutsi, Rwanda faced not only the physical devastation of infrastructure and communities but also the profound erosion of trust among its people. Rebuilding this trust, as the quote emphasizes, was an intricate and often painful endeavor, but it was also the linchpin for healing and progress.

Trust, as a foundation of any society, is fragile. When it shatters, as it did in Rwanda, the effects ripple through every facet of life. In the aftermath of immense trauma and betrayal, reestablishing trust seemed daunting, yet it was an absolute imperative for the nation's recovery. This lesson reminds us that rebuilding trust is a challenging but indispensable step on the path to healing and progress. Trust is a cornerstone of resilience, as it's trust that underpins the ability to cooperate, rebuild, and move forward. Without trust, reconciliation and unity remain elusive. The process of rebuilding trust requires individuals and communities to confront painful truths, acknowledge grievances, and, most challenging of all, extend forgiveness and understanding. It is a journey fraught with obstacles, yet the quote emphasizes that it's a journey worth undertaking.

This lesson is not confined to Rwanda; it reverberates globally. In a world marked by division, conflict, and breaches of trust, the importance of rebuilding trust remains universally significant. It's a reminder that the renewal of trust is not a one-time event but a continuous process, requiring ongoing dialogue, understanding, and a commitment to mend what's broken. The quote serves as an inspiring call to action, urging us to recognize that although the path of rebuilding trust may be difficult, it is indispensable for healing and progress. It underscores that the process of renewal is not only worthwhile but also a testament to the resilience of the human spirit. In Rwanda, trust was rebuilt step by step, serving as a testament to the capacity of humanity to heal, reconcile, and rekindle faith in one another.

Knowledge Empowers: "Education is the key that unlocks doors to empowerment and resilience."

This quote poignantly underscores the pivotal role of education in fostering empowerment and resilience. In the context of Rwanda's resilience journey, education emerged as a beacon of hope and a path to recovery. In the aftermath of the Genocide, a shattered nation recognized that the key to rebuilding lay in unlocking the doors to knowledge and understanding.

The quote encapsulates the idea that education is not merely about acquiring information but about empowerment. It equips individuals with the tools to make informed decisions, to gain a deeper understanding of the world, and to shape their own destinies. In the case of Rwanda, education was the gateway to empowerment for a populace that had experienced disempowerment on a devastating scale.

Education also serves as a powerful catalyst for resilience. Knowledge is the foundation upon which individuals and communities can build a more secure and prosperous future. Education equips people with problem-solving skills, critical thinking, and adaptability, all of which are vital in the face of adversity. It offers the means to recover from setbacks and to forge ahead with determination.

This lesson extends beyond the borders of Rwanda. It reminds us that education is an investment in individual and collective resilience. In a rapidly changing world where challenges and uncertainties abound, the key to empowerment and resilience lies in equipping people with the knowledge and skills they need to navigate and overcome obstacles.

Learning from History: "Remember the past to avoid repeating it, and to honor those who have suffered."

This quote beautifully encapsulates the essential lesson of the importance of learning from history, drawn from the Rwandan experience. The Genocide against the Tutsi left an indelible scar on the nation's history. It was a stark reminder of the devastating consequences of hatred, division, and violence. The quote serves as a poignant reminder that the past must be remembered not only to prevent its repetition but also to pay homage to those who endured unimaginable suffering. "Remember the past to avoid repeating it" underscores the idea that history is a teacher. It holds within it the lessons of humanity's gravest mistakes. To forget the past is to risk reliving it, and in the context of Rwanda, this is a lesson learned through heart-wrenching experience. By remembering the atrocities of the past, a nation can guard against the resurgence of hatred and violence, and work towards a more peaceful future. "Honor those who have suffered" is a call to recognize the resilience and strength of survivors and a tribute to those who lost their lives. It emphasizes that memory is not just about acknowledging the horrors but also about paying respect to the victims and their families. It is a way of preserving the dignity of those who endured immense suffering. The quote's lesson extends far beyond Rwanda. It is a universal reminder that history is a repository of wisdom. By studying and acknowledging the past, we can avoid repeating the mistakes that have led to unimaginable suffering and strife. It is a call for collective responsibility to ensure that the lessons of history are not forgotten. This quote serves as an inspiring call to action, urging us to remember history, not as a burden but as a guide. It is a testament to the strength of the human spirit to transform tragedy into lessons for a better future. It reminds us that by honoring the past, we pave the way for a more compassionate, enlightened, and peaceful world. The quote serves as an inspirational call to recognize the transformative power of education. It is a reminder that, even in the face of the most profound challenges, education is the key that can unlock doors to empowerment and resilience. It is a testament to the potential for individuals and societies to rise above adversity, armed with the tools and understanding that education provides.

Strong Leadership: "Effective leadership is essential for guiding a nation towards resilience."

This quote underlines the indispensable role of strong leadership in the context of fostering resilience, a vital lesson gleaned from the Rwandan experience. In the wake of the Genocide against the Tutsi, Rwanda faced an immense challenge that required a clear vision and strong leadership to navigate. The quote emphasizes that effective leadership is not merely advantageous but absolutely crucial in guiding a nation towards resilience.

At the heart of this message is the recognition that leadership provides direction, purpose, and unity. In the midst of chaos and devastation, effective leadership serves as the guiding force that empowers individuals and communities to overcome adversity. It offers the vision and determination to lead a nation out of despair and towards a more resilient future.

In Rwanda, leadership played a pivotal role in shaping the nation's recovery. It was the leaders who steered the course towards reconciliation, healing, and unity. They provided the stability and the vision that allowed Rwandans to rebuild their communities and their lives. This lesson emphasizes that, without strong leadership, the path to resilience becomes considerably more challenging.

The significance of strong leadership extends far beyond Rwanda's borders. It is a universal truth that applies to any nation facing adversity. Effective leadership can inspire individuals to come together, set a course for progress, and provide the unwavering support needed to overcome seemingly insurmountable challenges.

This quote serves as a reminder of the transformative power of leadership. It is an inspirational call to recognize that, even in the face of the most daunting challenges, strong and effective leadership can provide the guidance and motivation needed to navigate the path towards resilience. It highlights the critical role that leadership plays in shaping a nation's destiny, especially during times of crisis and recovery.

Empowering Women: "Empower women as key contributors to resilience and development."

This quote underscores the vital lesson that empowering women is not only a matter of gender equality but a fundamental strategy for building resilience and fostering development within a society. In the aftermath of the Genocide against the Tutsi in Rwanda, the nation recognized the importance of harnessing the potential of women as essential contributors to the process of rebuilding and healing.

The message conveyed by this quote is profound. It signifies that the empowerment of women is not an isolated objective; it is an investment in the resilience and progress of the entire community. Women, when empowered, bring a diverse range of perspectives, skills, and contributions to the table. They play a central role in the social fabric, and their involvement in decision-making processes can be transformative.

In Rwanda, women assumed leadership roles in politics, businesses, and community organizations, and their contributions were instrumental in the nation's journey towards resilience. Their active participation in rebuilding processes, their role in strengthening social bonds, and their commitment to education and healthcare played a significant part in the nation's recovery.

The lesson extends beyond Rwanda and serves as a universal reminder. It emphasizes that the advancement of women is not just a matter of justice but a pragmatic strategy for fostering resilience and development. In a world marked by complex challenges, empowering women is a key to innovation, adaptability, and progress.

This quote serves as an inspirational call to recognize the potential and power of women in society. It is a testament to the belief that, by empowering women and enabling their full participation in all aspects of life, we fortify the resilience and development of a community, a nation, and the world as a whole. It underscores the essential role that women play as architects of a more resilient and prosperous future.

Innovation's Triumph: "Innovation and adaptability can lead to breakthrough solutions."

This quote beautifully encapsulates the significance of innovation and adaptability as key drivers of resilience. In the wake of the Genocide against the Tutsi, the nation was confronted with an array of complex challenges, from social and economic rebuilding to healthcare and education. The quote emphasizes that it was the spirit of innovation and adaptability that led to the discovery of breakthrough solutions.

At its core, this message is a reminder that resilience is not solely about enduring adversity but also about finding creative ways to overcome it. Innovation is the capacity to think differently, to explore new ideas, and to adapt in the face of change. Adaptability is the ability to respond effectively to evolving circumstances. Together, they form a dynamic duo that leads to the development of new, more effective, and often transformative solutions.

In the case of Rwanda, innovation and adaptability were critical in various aspects of recovery. From the use of technology to improve healthcare services in remote areas to the development of sustainable agriculture practices, these qualities played a central role in driving the nation's progress. It was through innovative approaches and an adaptable mindset that breakthrough solutions emerged.

The lesson contained in this quote extends far beyond Rwanda. It is a universal truth that applies to any situation where resilience is needed. It highlights the potential for individuals and communities to navigate complex challenges by embracing innovation and adaptability as essential tools in their toolbox. This quote serves as an inspiring call to action, urging us to recognize that, in the face of adversity and uncertainty, the power of innovation and adaptability can lead to remarkable breakthroughs. It underscores that resilience is not a passive response but an active process of exploration and adaptation. It reminds us that, with the right mindset and approach, we have the potential to discover solutions that can transform our lives and the world.

Community's Support: "Community support is the foundation of our resilience. Together, we are unbeatable."

This quote underscores the immense importance of community support as the bedrock of resilience, a crucial lesson drawn from Rwanda's journey. In the aftermath of the Genocide against the Tutsi, where social bonds had been severely fractured, the quote emphasizes that the resilience of a nation is fundamentally rooted in the collective support and unity of its communities. At its core, this message reminds us that resilience is not a solitary endeavor but a collective one. In times of crisis, a strong and supportive community provides a safety net, a source of strength, and a framework for healing. Together, communities are able to pool resources, share burdens, and provide emotional and practical support that is essential for overcoming adversity.

In Rwanda, community support played a central role in the nation's recovery. Neighbors who had once been torn apart by violence came together to rebuild, reconcile, and forge a path towards a more peaceful future. It was within these communities that the bonds of trust and unity were strengthened, and resilience took root.

The lesson conveyed in this quote is universally significant. It is a reminder that, in a world marked by complex challenges and crises, the support and unity of communities are indispensable for resilience. It underscores that individuals and nations, when they come together, can face even the most formidable challenges with strength and determination.

This quote serves as an inspiring call to recognize the power of community. It is a testament to the belief that, in the face of adversity, we are at our strongest when we support one another, share our burdens, and work together towards a common goal. It emphasizes that, with the unwavering support of a community, we become an unstoppable force, capable of surmounting any obstacle and building a more resilient and united world.

Resilience is a Choice: "Resilience is a choice; individuals and nations can choose to overcome adversity."

This quote embodies the empowering message that resilience is not merely a circumstance or a product of luck but a conscious decision that individuals and nations can make in the face of adversity. It highlights the fundamental notion that, even when confronted with the most daunting challenges, the choice to be resilient is within our grasp.

At its core, this message is a reminder that resilience is not predetermined. It is a proactive response to adversity. It signifies that, even in the darkest of times, individuals and nations possess the agency to decide to rise above circumstances, to overcome adversity, and to chart a path towards recovery and renewal.

In the context of Rwanda, this choice was starkly evident. The nation, after enduring a harrowing Genocide, could have succumbed to despair and bitterness. However, Rwandans chose resilience. They chose to rebuild, reconcile, and forge a better future, despite the enormity of their challenges. This conscious choice became the driving force behind their healing and recovery.

The lesson contained in this quote extends far beyond Rwanda. It is a universal truth that applies to any situation where resilience is needed. It emphasizes that, regardless of the circumstances, the power to choose resilience is a potent one. It calls on individuals and nations to recognize their capacity for determination and their ability to rise above adversity.

This quote serves as an inspiring call to action, urging us to understand that, in the face of adversity, we have the choice to be resilient. It is a testament to the strength of the human spirit, the belief that, even when faced with the most challenging of situations, the choice to be resilient is within our reach. It underscores the idea that, by choosing resilience, individuals and nations can shape their destinies and create a more hopeful and resilient future.

Indomitable Spirit: "Never underestimate the strength and resilience of the human spirit."

This quote reverberates with the awe-inspiring message that the human spirit possesses a remarkable, even indomitable, strength and resilience that can surmount the most challenging circumstances. It serves as a reminder that the capacity for resilience within the human heart should never be underestimated.

At its core, this message emphasizes that the human spirit is not easily broken. Even when faced with unimaginable adversity, individuals can summon an inner strength and determination that enables them to endure, recover, and thrive. It underscores the idea that the human spirit is an unyielding force that refuses to be crushed by the weight of suffering and despair.

In the context of Rwanda, this message rings especially true. The nation's resilience in the aftermath of the Genocide against the Tutsi was a testament to the indomitable spirit of its people. Despite the depth of trauma and loss, Rwandans demonstrated that the human spirit can rise above darkness and forge a path towards healing and renewal.

The lesson contained in this quote extends beyond Rwanda's borders. It is a universal truth that applies to the human experience as a whole. It reminds us that, in the face of adversity, individuals possess an inherent strength and resilience that, when tapped into, can lead to remarkable feats of recovery and transformation.

This quote serves as an inspiring call to recognize the extraordinary resilience of the human spirit. It is a testament to the belief that, even in the face of the most profound challenges, the human spirit has the capacity to rise, to endure, and to triumph. It underscores the idea that, when we embrace the indomitable nature of the human spirit, we can overcome the most daunting of obstacles and create a future filled with hope and renewal.

Patience in Healing: "Healing takes time, and patience is a virtue in our journey toward recovery."

This quote emphasizes the vital lesson that healing, whether on an individual or societal level, is a process that unfolds over time. It underscores the idea that patience is not just a virtue but an essential attribute on the path to recovery and resilience.

At its core, this message reminds us that healing is not an instant fix; it's a journey. Whether dealing with personal trauma or the aftermath of a national tragedy, the process of recovery is marked by progress, setbacks, and, above all, time. Patience is the quality that enables individuals and communities to navigate this journey with grace and determination.

In the context of Rwanda, this message is particularly relevant. The nation's healing and recovery from the Genocide against the Tutsi were not achieved in a matter of days or even years. It was an ongoing process that required time and the cultivation of patience. Rwanda's experience serves as a poignant reminder that patience is the linchpin for reconciliation, understanding, and the rebuilding of lives and communities.

The lesson contained in this quote extends far beyond Rwanda. It is a universal truth that applies to the process of healing from any kind of adversity. It emphasizes that patience is a necessary component of resilience. It calls on individuals and nations to understand that, even in the face of profound challenges, patience is the guiding virtue that allows healing to occur. This quote serves as an inspiring call to action, urging us to recognize that, in the journey towards recovery, patience is the virtue that sustains us. It is a testament to the idea that, while resilience is marked by determination and action, patience is the quality that keeps us steadfast on the path to healing and renewal. It underscores the importance of understanding that, over time, healing is not only possible but probable when we possess the virtue of patience.

Reconciliation's Path: "Reconciliation is a continuous journey to mend divides and promote understanding."

This quote beautifully encapsulates the profound lesson that reconciliation is not a one-time event but an ongoing, dynamic process. It emphasizes that reconciliation is not only about bridging divides but also about nurturing a deeper understanding among individuals and communities.

At its core, this message reminds us that reconciliation is a commitment to healing and unity. It signifies that, even in the face of deeply entrenched differences and past grievances, the path to reconciliation is an enduring one. It calls for a continuous effort to mend divides, promote empathy, and build bridges that bring people together.

In the context of Rwanda, this message is particularly poignant. The nation's journey toward reconciliation after the Genocide was not a swift or simple endeavor. It required a sustained commitment to understanding, forgiveness, and the healing of both survivors and those who had perpetrated acts of violence. Rwanda serves as a testament to the belief that reconciliation is a journey that demands patience and unwavering effort.

The lesson contained in this quote extends far beyond Rwanda's borders. It is a universal truth that applies to any situation where reconciliation is needed. It emphasizes that reconciliation is not a destination but a path to follow. It is a call to recognize that, in a world marked by division and conflict, the journey of reconciliation is one that should be sustained and nurtured over time.

This quote serves as an inspiring call to action, urging us to understand that reconciliation is an ongoing journey. It is a testament to the belief that, even in the face of the most profound divides, reconciliation is not only possible but necessary. It underscores the idea that, through continuous effort and understanding, we can heal wounds, mend divides, and promote a more united and compassionate world.

Global Solidarity: "International solidarity is a testament to humanity's potential. The world can support nations in need."

This quote highlights the essential lesson that international solidarity is a demonstration of the collective potential of humanity. It underscores the idea that, in a world interconnected by technology and communication, nations have the capacity to support one another in times of need.

At its core, this message reminds us that, as inhabitants of a global community, we are not isolated entities but interconnected parts of a whole. International solidarity signifies that, when a nation faces crises or challenges, the world has the ability to come together and offer support, whether in terms of humanitarian aid, resources, or simply empathy.

In the context of Rwanda's experience, this message is particularly meaningful. The nation, in the aftermath of the Genocide, received international support that played a crucial role in its healing and recovery. The global response to Rwanda's crisis serves as a testament to the belief that, even in the face of immense suffering, the world has the potential to provide assistance and solidarity.

The lesson contained in this quote extends far beyond Rwanda's borders. It is a universal truth that applies to any situation where nations face adversity. It emphasizes that global solidarity is not just a concept but a tangible and essential means of offering support to those in need. It calls on nations to recognize that, in a world marked by challenges, the potential for international cooperation and solidarity is an invaluable resource.

This quote serves as an inspiring call to action, urging us to understand that international solidarity is a testament to humanity's capacity for compassion and unity. It is a reminder that, even in the face of the most challenging circumstances, the world can come together to provide support and assistance. It underscores the idea that, through global solidarity, nations in need can find hope, strength, and the means to overcome adversity.

Balance in Remembering: "Balancing remembering the lost with building a better future is vital."

This quote conveys a poignant lesson about the delicate balance between honoring the past and forging a brighter future. It emphasizes that, when confronted with a history marked by loss and tragedy, finding equilibrium between remembering those who were lost and actively working towards a better future is of paramount importance.

At its core, this message reminds us that, while it's essential to acknowledge the pain and suffering of the past, it's equally vital to channel that remembrance into constructive action. It signifies that, even in the face of profound grief and loss, we must not be paralyzed by the past but motivated to create a future marked by healing, growth, and hope.

In the context of Rwanda, this message holds profound significance. The nation, after the Genocide against Tutsi, faced the challenge of remembering the hundreds of thousands who had perished while striving to rebuild a more peaceful and unified future. Rwanda serves as a testament to the belief that, by finding the equilibrium between remembrance and progress, nations can transform tragedy into a catalyst for positive change.

The lesson contained in this quote extends far beyond Rwanda's borders. It is a universal truth that applies to any situation where the past is marked by loss and adversity. It emphasizes the importance of recognizing that, even in the face of the most painful history, we can find inspiration and motivation to build a better world.

This quote serves as an inspiring call to action, urging us to understand that the balance between remembrance and progress is vital. It is a testament to the belief that, in the face of profound loss, we have the capacity to honor the past by creating a future marked by compassion, unity, and resilience. It underscores the idea that, through this balance, we can transform tragedy into a driving force for positive change.

Persistence Pays Off: "Perseverance and determination lead to positive results over time."

This quote encapsulates the essential lesson that perseverance and determination are key ingredients for achieving positive outcomes in the long run. It emphasizes that success and resilience are often the fruits of sustained effort and unwavering commitment.

At its core, this message reminds us that, when faced with adversity or complex challenges, giving up is not the answer. Instead, it encourages individuals and nations to recognize that, through continued dedication and resilience, they can work towards positive change and transformation over time.

In the context of Rwanda, this lesson is particularly poignant. The nation's journey towards healing and recovery was marked by persistent efforts to rebuild communities, reconcile divides, and foster unity. Rwanda serves as a testament to the belief that, even in the face of seemingly insurmountable obstacles, perseverance and determination can lead to remarkable positive results.

The lesson contained in this quote extends far beyond Rwanda's borders. It is a universal truth that applies to any situation where resilience is needed. It emphasizes that, even when faced with the most challenging circumstances, individuals and nations have the capacity to achieve meaningful and positive results by persistently working towards their goals.

This quote serves as an inspiring call to action, urging us to understand that, in the journey of resilience and positive change, persistence is the key. It is a testament to the belief that, with unwavering determination and a commitment to long-term goals, individuals and nations can achieve remarkable results, even in the face of the most daunting challenges. It underscores the idea that, through persistence, we can create a future marked by success and resilience.

Bridge Divides: "Empathy and compassion can bridge gaps and promote understanding."

This quote conveys a powerful lesson about the transformative potential of empathy and compassion in healing societal divides and fostering understanding. It underscores that, in a world often marked by differences and conflict, these qualities can serve as bridges that connect people and promote a deeper sense of unity.

At its core, this message reminds us that, even in the face of deep-seated divisions, the capacity for empathy and compassion can lead to reconciliation and healing. It signifies that these qualities have the ability to soften hearts, create common ground, and build bridges that allow individuals and communities to move beyond their differences.

In the context of Rwanda, this message is particularly significant. The nation's journey towards healing and reconciliation following the Genocide was marked by the cultivation of empathy and compassion. Rwanda serves as a testament to the belief that, even when faced with the most profound of divides, these qualities can bridge gaps and pave the way for understanding and unity.

The lesson contained in this quote extends far beyond Rwanda's borders. It is a universal truth that applies to any situation where divisions exist. It emphasizes that empathy and compassion are not just abstract ideals but tangible tools for building bridges and fostering a more harmonious and compassionate world.

This quote serves as an inspiring call to action, urging us to recognize the transformative power of empathy and compassion. It is a testament to the belief that, even in the face of seemingly insurmountable divides, these qualities can bridge gaps and create pathways to understanding and unity. It underscores the idea that, through empathy and compassion, we can heal wounds, build bridges, and promote a world marked by empathy, compassion, and resilience.

Belief in Tomorrow: "Faith in a better future guides our actions, propelling us forward."

This quote embodies the powerful lesson that faith in a brighter tomorrow is a driving force that propels individuals and nations forward. It emphasizes that belief in a better future serves as a guiding light, motivating actions that lead to progress, healing, and resilience.

At its core, this message reminds us that, even in the face of adversity, maintaining hope and faith in a positive future is not just a passive sentiment but an active force for change. It signifies that this belief is a catalyst that empowers individuals and communities to take actions that create the better world they envision.

In the context of Rwanda, this lesson holds profound significance. The nation's journey towards resilience was marked by a collective belief in a more peaceful and unified future. Rwanda serves as a testament to the belief that, even in the wake of immense tragedy, the conviction in a brighter tomorrow can guide actions that lead to healing and progress.

The lesson contained in this quote extends far beyond Rwanda's borders. It is a universal truth that applies to any situation where individuals or nations face adversity. It emphasizes that, even when confronted with profound challenges, maintaining faith in a better future is not just a form of optimism but a source of strength and determination.

This quote serves as an inspiring call to action, urging us to understand that belief in a better tomorrow is a guiding force that propels us forward. It is a testament to the belief that, even in the face of the most daunting challenges, faith in a brighter future can inspire actions that create a more hopeful, resilient, and compassionate world. It underscores the idea that, through belief and action, we can shape the destiny of individuals, communities, and nations.

Environmental Responsibility: "Protecting the environment is essential for long-term resilience."

This quote conveys a crucial lesson that environmental responsibility is a foundational element in ensuring the long-term resilience of individuals, communities, and nations. It emphasizes that safeguarding the environment is not merely an ecological concern but a fundamental aspect of our ability to endure and thrive.

At its core, this message reminds us that the environment plays a pivotal role in sustaining life and providing resources necessary for resilience. It signifies that responsible environmental stewardship is an investment in the future, as it safeguards the ecosystems that offer vital services like clean air, water, and fertile land for agriculture.

In the context of Rwanda, this lesson is particularly significant. The nation's commitment to environmental sustainability, including reforestation and conservation efforts, played a role in its journey towards resilience. Rwanda serves as a testament to the belief that protecting the environment is not just a matter of ecological ethics but a practical approach to ensuring a sustainable future.

The lesson contained in this quote extends far beyond Rwanda's borders. It is a universal truth that applies to every corner of the globe. It emphasizes that, in an era marked by environmental challenges and climate change, the responsibility to protect and preserve our environment is paramount for our collective resilience.

This quote serves as an inspiring call to action, urging us to understand that environmental responsibility is inextricably linked to our resilience as individuals, communities, and nations. It is a testament to the belief that, by caring for the environment, we secure the foundation for our long-term well-being and the ability to endure and flourish in the face of a changing world. It underscores the idea that, through responsible environmental practices, we pave the way for a resilient and sustainable future.

Mental Fortitude: "Cultivating mental strength and positivity is crucial in facing adversity."

This quote imparts a significant lesson about the importance of mental resilience and a positive mindset in confronting and surmounting adversity. It emphasizes that the fortitude of the human mind plays a critical role in overcoming challenges and building resilience.

At its core, this message reminds us that, while external factors and circumstances may pose formidable challenges, it is our mental strength and attitude that can determine our ability to overcome them. It signifies that cultivating a resilient mindset, characterized by optimism and determination, is a powerful tool in navigating difficult times.

In the context of Rwanda, this lesson is especially meaningful. The nation's journey towards recovery and resilience required not only physical rebuilding but also the mental fortitude to heal from the deep wounds of the past. Rwanda serves as a testament to the belief that, even in the aftermath of immense tragedy, the human spirit can be fortified through mental strength and a positive outlook.

The lesson contained in this quote extends far beyond Rwanda's borders. It is a universal truth that applies to any situation where individuals or communities face adversity. It emphasizes that, regardless of the challenges, a resilient mindset can be cultivated and nurtured, empowering us to respond to difficulties with courage and hope.

This quote serves as an inspiring call to action, urging us to understand that mental fortitude and positivity are essential assets in the face of adversity. It is a testament to the belief that, through mental strength and a positive outlook, we can confront challenges with unwavering determination and resilience. It underscores the idea that, by cultivating resilience within our minds, we have the power to shape our responses to adversity and create a brighter future.

Youth Empowerment: "Engaging and empowering youth is an investment in a resilient future."

This quote conveys a profound lesson about the critical role of engaging and empowering the youth in shaping a resilient future for individuals, communities, and nations. It emphasizes that investing in the younger generation is not just an act of support but a strategic measure to ensure enduring strength and adaptability.

At its core, this message reminds us that young people represent the future. By providing them with opportunities, education, and a sense of agency, we are investing in the collective resilience of our society. It signifies that the energy, creativity, and determination of youth are powerful assets that can drive positive change and propel us through future challenges.

In the context of Rwanda, this lesson is particularly significant. The nation's emphasis on youth empowerment and education played a vital role in its recovery and resilience. Rwanda serves as a testament to the belief that, by engaging and empowering the youth, we create a resilient foundation that can withstand future adversities.

The lesson contained in this quote extends far beyond Rwanda's borders. It is a universal truth that applies to every society where young people hold the potential to shape the future. It emphasizes that by supporting and empowering the youth, we are not only preparing them for leadership but also securing the resilience and adaptability of our communities and nations.

This quote serves as an inspiring call to action, urging us to understand that youth empowerment is an investment in the resilience of our future. It is a testament to the belief that, by nurturing the potential of young individuals, we are cultivating the leaders, innovators, and change-makers who will guide us through challenges with vigor and determination. It underscores the idea that, through youth empowerment, we are creating a resilient, vibrant, and promising future.

Creativity's Healing Touch: "Art, music, and culture bring healing and joy even in challenging times."

This quote imparts a profound lesson about the therapeutic power of art, music, and culture in times of adversity. It emphasizes that creativity and expression are not only sources of joy but also potent tools for healing and resilience when faced with challenging circumstances.

At its core, this message reminds us that the human spirit is nourished by the arts and culture. In moments of difficulty, these forms of expression serve as a means of catharsis and inspiration. They provide solace, hope, and a sense of connection, allowing individuals and communities to find strength and healing through the arts.

In the context of Rwanda, this lesson is particularly poignant. The nation's embrace of art, music, and culture as mechanisms for healing and reconciliation is a testament to their capacity to bring solace and unity even in the aftermath of immense tragedy. Rwanda serves as a reminder that, amidst the darkest of times, creativity can be a beacon of hope.

The lesson contained in this quote extends far beyond Rwanda's borders. It is a universal truth that applies to any situation where individuals and communities face adversity. It emphasizes that, through creative expression, people can find comfort, resilience, and a sense of purpose in their lives.

This quote serves as an inspiring call to action, urging us to recognize the healing power of art, music, and culture. It is a testament to the belief that, even in the face of the most challenging circumstances, these forms of expression have the potential to bring joy, healing, and a sense of unity. It underscores the idea that, through creativity's healing touch, we can navigate adversity with grace, inspire resilience, and create a world filled with beauty and hope.

Never Giving Up: "Resilience is an ongoing journey; setbacks are part of the process."

This quote imparts a vital lesson about the continuous nature of resilience. It emphasizes that the path to resilience is not linear; rather, it is an ongoing journey marked by progress, setbacks, and the unwavering commitment to never give up.

At its core, this message reminds us that resilience is not a destination but a way of life. It signifies that the journey towards resilience is characterized by determination, adaptability, and the resilience to persevere, even in the face of setbacks and challenges.

In the context of Rwanda, this lesson is particularly poignant. The nation's experience of recovery and healing after the Genocide was far from straightforward. It was marked by hurdles and difficulties that required resilience and a commitment to the ongoing journey of rebuilding. Rwanda serves as a testament to the belief that, even when faced with setbacks, the choice to never give up can lead to remarkable transformation and growth.

The lesson contained in this quote extends far beyond Rwanda's borders. It is a universal truth that applies to any situation where individuals or communities encounter adversity. It emphasizes that, in the face of challenges, resilience is not about avoiding setbacks but about learning from them and continuing to move forward with unwavering determination.

This quote serves as an inspiring call to action, urging us to understand that resilience is an ongoing journey, and setbacks are inherent to the process. It is a testament to the belief that, even in the face of difficulties, the commitment to never give up is the key to enduring resilience. It underscores the idea that, through the understanding that setbacks are part of the journey, we can persevere, grow stronger, and create a future marked by resilience and hope.

Love Conquers: "Love and compassion can conquer hatred and cruelty."

This quote imparts a profound lesson about the transformative power of love and compassion in the face of hatred and cruelty. It emphasizes that these positive emotions have the capacity to transcend negativity, promoting healing, reconciliation, and resilience.

At its core, this message reminds us that, even in the face of the darkest of human behaviors, the light of love and compassion can dispel the shadows of hatred and cruelty. It signifies that these emotions hold the potential to bridge divides, foster understanding, and mend wounds.

In the context of Rwanda, this lesson is particularly poignant. The nation's journey towards healing and reconciliation after the Genocide was underpinned by the embrace of love and compassion. Rwanda serves as a testament to the belief that, even when confronted with the depths of human cruelty, these positive emotions can emerge as powerful forces that bring about forgiveness, unity, and resilience.

The lesson contained in this quote extends far beyond Rwanda's borders. It is a universal truth that applies to any situation where individuals or communities face hatred and cruelty. It emphasizes that, through the cultivation of love and compassion, we have the ability to conquer darkness and create a world marked by empathy, unity, and resilience.

This quote serves as an inspiring call to action, urging us to recognize that love and compassion are forces capable of conquering even the most profound hatred and cruelty. It is a testament to the belief that, in the face of negativity, these emotions are not just fleeting sentiments but powerful agents of change and healing. It underscores the idea that, through love and compassion, we can rise above adversity, mend the deepest of divisions, and foster a world filled with hope, understanding, and resilience.

Non-Violence Prevails: "Peaceful means can bring about profound change and healing."

This quote conveys a profound lesson about the enduring power of non-violence in effecting transformative change and healing. It emphasizes that peaceful methods, even in the face of conflict and adversity, have the capacity to bring about profound positive shifts in society.

At its core, this message reminds us that violence is not the only path to change. It signifies that non-violent approaches, such as dialogue, negotiation, and reconciliation, can lead to healing, understanding, and the resolution of deep-seated issues. It underscores the idea that the absence of violence is not merely the absence of conflict but the presence of peaceful and constructive means to address challenges.

In the context of Rwanda, this lesson is especially poignant. The nation's journey towards healing and reconciliation after the Genocide was marked by a commitment to non-violence. Rwanda serves as a testament to the belief that, even in the wake of extreme violence, peaceful means can prevail and lead to profound change and healing.

The lesson contained in this quote extends far beyond Rwanda's borders. It is a universal truth that applies to any situation where conflict and adversity exist. It emphasizes that, regardless of the circumstances, non-violent approaches are not just a moral ideal but a practical and effective way to foster resilience, understanding, and lasting peace.

This quote serves as an inspiring call to action, urging us to understand that non-violence prevails in its ability to bring about profound change and healing. It is a testament to the belief that, in the face of conflict and adversity, peaceful means are not signs of weakness but sources of strength and resilience. It underscores the idea that, through non-violence, we can transform societies, resolve conflicts, and build a world marked by enduring peace and unity.

Inspiring from Despair: "From Rwanda, the world learns that even in the face of despair, we can rebuild, thrive, and love."

This quote conveys a deeply inspirational lesson about the incredible capacity of the human spirit to rise from the depths of despair and create a future filled with hope, resilience, and love. It emphasizes that, even in the darkest of times, there is an inherent ability within individuals and communities to rebuild, not just surviving but thriving, and to cultivate love as a powerful force for healing.

At its core, this message reminds us that despair is not the final chapter of the story. It signifies that, even in the face of unimaginable tragedy, there is a wellspring of strength that can be tapped into to rebuild shattered lives and societies. It underscores the idea that love and resilience can emerge as guiding lights to lead us away from the darkest corners of despair. In the context of Rwanda, this lesson is incredibly moving. The nation's history, marked by the Genocide, is a testament to the belief that, from the depths of despair, a remarkable journey of recovery, rebuilding, and reconciliation is possible. Rwanda serves as an inspiring example to the world that, even in the face of the most profound despair, individuals and communities can find the strength to rebuild, thrive, and love again.

The lesson contained in this quote extends far beyond Rwanda's borders. It is a universal truth that applies to any situation where despair exists. It emphasizes that, no matter the circumstances, hope and resilience can shine through. It calls on individuals and communities to recognize that even in the darkest of moments, the human spirit can emerge stronger, and love can be the guiding force to heal and create a brighter future. This quote serves as an inspiring call to action, urging us to understand that despair is not the end, but a new beginning. It is a testament to the belief that, even in the face of seemingly insurmountable despair, the human spirit can overcome, rebuild, thrive, and, most importantly, love. It underscores the idea that, through this resilience and love, we can inspire and uplift individuals, communities, and nations worldwide.

Lessons for the World: "The principles of resilience transcend borders and can be applied worldwide."

This quote imparts a profound lesson that the principles of resilience are not confined by geographical or cultural boundaries; they are universal and can be employed across the globe. It emphasizes that the core values and strategies that enable individuals and nations to overcome adversity can serve as guiding lights for people everywhere.

At its core, this message reminds us that the journey of resilience is a shared human experience. The principles that underpin resilience, such as determination, unity, empathy, and hope, are common to us all. It signifies that these principles can transcend borders and offer lessons to individuals, communities, and nations, regardless of their backgrounds or circumstances.

In the context of Rwanda, this lesson serves as a testament to the universal nature of resilience. The nation's journey towards healing and recovery, while unique to its history, carries lessons that resonate with people worldwide. Rwanda's experience showcases the belief that the principles of resilience, when applied diligently, can lead to profound transformation and progress.

The lesson contained in this quote extends far beyond Rwanda's borders. It is a universal truth that is relevant to any situation where people strive to overcome adversity. It emphasizes that the principles of resilience, such as unity, compassion, and determination, are not bound by specific contexts but can offer guidance and inspiration on a global scale.

This quote serves as an inspiring call to action, urging us to understand that the principles of resilience are shared by humanity as a whole. It is a testament to the belief that, when we recognize and apply these principles, we can face challenges with strength and determination, fostering resilience and creating a better world for everyone. It underscores the idea that, through these shared principles, we can connect and uplift individuals, communities, and nations across the world.

Over the past 30 years, Rwanda's journey of resilience from the ashes of the Genocide has yielded 30 profound lessons for the world. These lessons, ranging from unity and forgiveness to non-violence and love, reflect the enduring strength of the human spirit. Rwanda's story serves as an inspirational testament to the transformative power of resilience and the ability to rebuild, thrive, and love even in the face of unimaginable adversity. The nation's commitment to unity, education, and environmental responsibility, as well as its unwavering belief in a better future, exemplifies that resilience is not only a choice but a conscious decision to create a brighter and more compassionate world. Rwanda's resilience is a beacon of hope that continues to guide and inspire the global community.

Thank you!

I want to express my deepest gratitude to each and every one of you who have embarked on this journey through the pages of this book with me. It has been a dream that I nurtured for two long years, and your presence here makes it all the more special. Together, we have delved into the profound lessons of resilience that Rwanda has offered to the world.

My purpose in writing this book was twofold: not only did I aspire to inspire you, the readers, and people around the globe to bounce back from adversity, but I also wanted to pay tribute to Rwanda. The remarkable journey of resilience that this nation has undertaken is a beacon of hope and a powerful definition of what it means to rise from the ashes. Rwanda's unwavering spirit and commitment to unity, forgiveness, and love are lessons that the world can cherish and emulate.

As you close the final pages of this book, I wish you all the best in your own personal journeys. May you find the strength and inspiration to rebound in the face of any difficulty or challenge that comes your way. Let Rwanda's example be a constant reminder that resilience is not only a choice but a testament to the incredible fortitude of the human spirit. Thank you once again for sharing this journey with me, and may your path ahead be marked by resilience, hope, and an unwavering spirit to overcome.

Acknowledgement

I am profoundly grateful to my family, the bedrock of my resilience, for their unwavering support. To my friends, you've been my pillars of strength. My heartfelt thanks to the professionals who graciously reviewed my book Eric Mahoro, Rev canon Dr. Antoine Rutayisire, Dr. Chaste Uwihoreye, Dr. Gakwenzire Philbert, Nkuranga Jean Pierre, Dr. Ryarasa Nkurunziza, Ndungutse Theoneste and the research team in MINUBUMWE.

Special appreciation to the encouraging authors: Judence Kayitesi, Omar Ndizeye, Dimitrie Sissi, Charles Habonimana. A heartfelt acknowledgment to Dr. Ndushabandi Eric for his mentorship and inspiring foreword. And immense gratitude to the organizations, especially AERG, RNSA, NAR, for their unwavering partnership.

Last but not least, a big thank you to Inzozi Publisher for nurturing the manuscript into an amazing piece of art.

Aspire to rebounce

Be Rwanda and always shine after the darkness

Embark on a profound journey in **Rebounce: Transgenerational Resilience** in Rwanda, where you'll witness Rwanda's remarkable resilience in the face of adversity. This emotionally charged narrative redefines what it means to overcome challenges, offering lessons in unity, forgiveness, and hope. The book reveals the ingredients of resilience, explores the transgenerational transfer of strength, and showcases the conscious choice to rebound from adversity. Through Rwanda's story, you'll find inspiration to conquer your own challenges.

As you close the final page, remember that resilience is a testament to the incredible fortitude of the human spirit.

Aspire to rebounce,
Be Rwanda, and always
Shine after the darkness.

REFERENCES

1.   Bonanno, G. A. (2004). Loss, trauma, and human resilience: Have we underestimated the human capacity to thrive after extremely aversive events? American Psychologist, 59(1), 20–28.

2.   Masten, A. S. (2001). Ordinary magic: Resilience processes in development. American Psychologist, 56(3), 227–238.

3.   Ungar, M. (2011). The social ecology of resilience: A handbook of theory and practice. Springer Science & Business Media.

4.   Luthar, S. S., Cicchetti, D., & Becker, B. (2000). The construct of resilience: A critical evaluation and guidelines for future work. Child Development, 71(3), 543–562.

5.   Tedeschi, R. G., & Calhoun, L. G. (2004). Posttraumatic growth: Conceptual foundations and empirical evidence. Psychological Inquiry, 15(1), 1–18.

6.   Snyder, C. R., & Lopez, S. J. (2009). Oxford handbook of positive psychology. Oxford University Press.

7.   Rwanda Governance Board. (2019). Imihigo.

8.   Kagame, P. (2003). Rwanda's rebirth: Challenges ahead. Foreign Affairs, 82(6), 14–27.

9.   Southwick, S. M., & Charney, D. S. (2012). Resilience: The science of mastering life's greatest challenges. Cambridge University Press.

10.   Masten, A. S., & Narayan, A. J. (2012). Child development in the context of disaster, war, and terrorism: Pathways of risk and resilience. Annual Review of Psychology, 63, 227-257.

11.   Seligman, M. E. P. (2011). Flourish: A visionary new understanding of happiness and well-being. Free Press.

12.   Fredrickson, B. L. (2001). The role of positive emotions in positive psychology: The broaden-and-build theory of positive emotions. American Psychologist, 56(3), 218-226.

13.   Fredrickson, B. L. (2004). Gratitude, like other positive emotions, broadens and builds. The psychology of gratitude, 145-166.

14.   Deci, E. L., & Ryan, R. M. (2000). The" what" and" why" of goal pursuits: Human needs and the self-determination of behavior. Psychological Inquiry, 11(4), 227-268.

15.   Almedom, A. M. (2005). Resilience, hardiness, sense of coherence, and posttraumatic growth: All paths leading to" light at the end of the tunnel"?. Journal of Loss and Trauma, 10(3), 253-265.

16.   Rutter, M. (2006). Implications of resilience concepts for scientific understanding. Annals of the New York Academy of Sciences, 1094(1), 1-12.

17.   Masten, A. S., & Obradović, J. (2006). Competence and resilience in development. Annals of the New York Academy of Sciences, 1094(1), 13-27.

18.   Bonanno, G. A. (2005). Resilience in the face of potential trauma. Current Directions in Psychological Science, 14(3), 135-138.

19.   Reivich, K., & Shatte, A. (2002). The resilience factor: 7 keys to finding your inner strength and overcoming life's hurdles. Harmony.